P9-BZQ-658

Strangling Your Husband Is **NOT** an Option

A Practical Guide to Dramatically Improving Your Marriage

Merrilee Browne Boyack

DESERET BOOK

Salt Lake City, Utah

This book is dedicated to my mom, Hilda Faulkner Browne,
my first teacher on how to be a wife.

© 2006 Merrilee Boyack

All rights reserved. No part of this book may be reproduced in any form or by any means without permission in writing from the publisher, Deseret Book Company, P. O. Box 30178, Salt Lake City, Utah 84130. This work is not an official publication of The Church of Jesus Christ of Latter-day Saints. The views expressed herein are the responsibility of the author and do not necessarily represent the position of the Church or of Deseret Book Company.

DESERET BOOK is a registered trademark of Deseret Book Company.

Visit us at deseretbook.com

Library of Congress Cataloging-in-Publication Data

Boyack, Merrilee Browne.
    Strangling your husband is not an option : a practical guide to dramatically improving your marriage / Merrilee Browne Boyack.
        p.   cm.
    Includes index.
    ISBN-10 1-59038-582-9 (pbk.)
    ISBN-13 978-1-59038-582-1 (pbk.)
    1. Marriage—Handbooks, manuals, etc. 2. Man-woman relationships—Handbooks, manuals, etc. 3. Wives—Conduct of life. I. Title.
HQ734.B775 2006
248.8'4350882893—dc22   2006001882

Printed in the United States of America

10   9   8   7   6   5   4   3   2   1

Contents

Preface

This book took a lot of courage to write. It's a rather sensitive topic for each of us—including me. I'd truly like to thank my husband, Steve, who encouraged me and was brave enough to be a part of this. It has been such an honor to be his wife for over twenty-six years. I'm not sure he knew what he was getting into, but he has hung in there regardless. Bless him for his courage and patience.

I'd like to thank my mom, Hilda Faulkner Browne, who taught me my first lessons in the real world of living as a wife day-to-day—and who didn't laugh too hard when I told her I was writing this. And as always, thanks to my personal Ya-Ya's, Diane, Sue, and Libby, who always believe in me and support me and don't fall down laughing at all my wild ideas.

CHAPTER 1

Getting Started

Learning and growing is an exciting prospect.
Changing how we act and who we are as wives is
a thrilling adventure.

I have a very small confession to make: I am not quite the perfect wife yet. Almost, but not quite. And I figure after a few
hundred more years, I will definitely be there. Until that
point, I am a work in progress just like you. But after a quarter
century of marriage (Holy Toledo! That sounds interminably
long!), I have learned a few things about being a wife. Most I've
learned the hard way.

There are so many things that I wish I had known when I
was a new young wife. But I am grateful that I have learned so
much in the first twenty-six years, and I feel a desire to share it
with others who desire to improve their own marriages. I'm sure
there is a ton more to learn in the decades to come, and I'm
excited by those prospects.

Now I know that you're still chuckling over the title of this
book. I must admit I was very surprised when it was suggested
by my publisher. He commented, "But Merrilee, it fits your personality!" I assured him that while I agree that it did mirror my

own warped sense of humor, I wasn't so sure it should be put on the cover! My mother-in-law was concerned that it reflected poorly on her son, but I assured her that it did not reference my dear husband specifically. I assured her that *many* (dare I say most?) wives are sometimes exasperated with their dear husbands.

So let us keep in mind that we shall *not* be recommending strangling as a good option for improving our marriages! (Much to the relief of our hubbies, I am sure.)

As I contemplated this subject of being a wife, I realized that there are many types of wives out there. Some are good; some are great; some are lousy. Some wives are gifted communicators. Others are amazing nurturers. All in all, however, I realized early on that I would not be like any other wife. I may not be great, good, perfect, or anything like anyone else. But the one thing I could do was to be *smart*. I could learn what works well and try to apply it to my own marriage. I could also learn what was not effective and try to eliminate it. Each of us can strive, within our own unique situations and with our own unique abilities, to be a smart wife.

Have you noticed that there aren't too many classes and very few books on being a wife? That's because no guy on the planet would stand up and tell a group of women how to do it. And frankly, very few women have the guts to do it either. But I'm very much in touch with my faults, so I'm okay with talking about it while realizing that I'm still working on it.

I truly owe a debt of gratitude to those who have helped me learn how to be a better wife, particularly my older sister. So just for purposes of this book, I'll be your older sister—but a very young-looking older sister!

This topic—improving ourselves as wives—goes directly to one of the most important issues of our day. Listen to President Gordon B. Hinckley's comments. When a reporter asked him about his greatest concerns, President Hinckley replied, "I am concerned about family life in the Church. We have wonderful people, but we have too many whose families are falling apart. It is a matter of serious concern. I think it is my most serious concern."[1] That is rather frank and scary coming from our prophet. Anything we can do to improve ourselves as wives and to improve our marriages is vitally important.

Now think about being a wife. A wife is not her husband's mother (although some act that way); she's not his daughter; she's not always even his best friend. She's his wife. What does that mean?

At Sunday School a teacher explained how God created everything, including human beings. Little Johnny seemed especially intent when they told him how Eve was created out of one of Adam's ribs. Later in the week his mother noticed him lying down as though he were ill and said, "Johnny, what is the matter?" Little Johnny responded, "I have a pain in my side. I think I'm going to have a wife."

That may be how some husbands view us—as a pain in the side. But hopefully we (and they) have a better view of who we are.

But how do you learn how to be a wife? How do you incorporate that new role into your life? That's not particularly easy to do. And most women are reluctant—because of fear or embarrassment—to discuss how they're developing as a wife.

Can you just envision being out to lunch with your female friends and having this conversation? "So, how are you doing as a wife?" "Oh, well, I'm doing a great job on the supporting aspect but I'm lousy at that whole communications thing." Right. Like that would ever happen. Most of our interactions with other women center around homemaking, children, work, and other safe topics. Any discussion about our marriages tends to focus on the collective husband-bashing that has practically become the sport of choice for groups of women across the nation.

Part of this stems from the difficulty many women have in admitting imperfection. Some women would rather have their tongue cut out than admit that they need help learning how to be a better wife or that they are making mistakes. Such an admission would damage the façade many of us spend so much time carefully constructing. I believe that this does more damage than good. We go around feeling depressed because all we see is the plastic image others hold up for the world. And we know that we fall far short of their image and our pretend image as well. No wonder we're depressed!

Yet it should surprise no one to learn that their friends are having a hard time getting their husbands to talk to them or help around the house. They're frustrated with themselves, and they're frustrated with the struggle of handling a marriage, just like you. We just need to be more open in admitting that struggle and asking for help.

But asking for help with being a wife is tricky business. We may want to ask for input, but we also want to protect the privacy and sanctity of our marriages. That makes for a challenging situation.

We need to move forward anyway. I'm going to take a deep breath and talk to you about what it means to be a wife. I'll be very real and very honest, which is making my husband nervous. It takes a brave husband to support his wife in writing a book like this, and I appreciate his courage. He will be reading (and editing) the book first to protect his reputation. But I truly appreciate his willingness to share. I will not be glossing over the ups and downs that we all experience. You'll also hear stories from women I've met, with guts, feathers, and all. That is why I will be changing virtually every name in this book to protect their privacy as well.

My sister once asked me a question that she asks in her Marriage and Family Relations class: "If you were dead and your husband was looking for another wife, would he pick you?"

Now that's a rather tough question to consider. I had to look at my slightly expanded waistline, expanded thighs, drooping posterior region, and all the ravages of gravity and gray hairs and wonder, Would he? But now think about the person you've become—the things you've learned, the strength you've gained—and look at that question again. Would he? If there are things we need to fix, then let's get on it. If there are areas where we would like to improve, then let's be open enough to learn about them and then try to take some steps to make those changes.

Learning and growing is an exciting prospect. Changing how we act and who we are as wives is a thrilling adventure.

But before we begin, we must take the Dump the Guilt Pledge. This is always crucial to taking these first steps. So raise your right hand. . . . I'm waiting. Put it up there. Okay, now repeat after me: "I pledge . . . " Wait a minute. Let's do this better. "I, the fabulous, wonderful, charming, and brilliant person that I am [feel free to embellish at will], do hereby pledge that I will not focus on any mistakes that I have made in the past. I pledge that I will not go around feeling all mopey and depressed and think, 'Gee, why didn't I do this sooner?' or any other stupid notions. I pledge that I will face forward and just try to focus on improving from this day forward and that I will dump any and all guilt I've been dragging around in the past."

There, now, don't you feel better? Now we can begin.

Listen to the Spirit

As we proceed, I would like to emphasize one critical principle that needs to be woven through every bit of advice and suggestions and ideas that I give you in this book. The Holy

Ghost will help you know what to focus on in your marriage. He will help you know what to apply and what to set aside. Listen to the Spirit. Listen keenly and intently. Ponder everything you learn and what you're prompted to do. Heavenly Father knows you better than you know yourself. He loves you dearly, and He loves your husband. He knows what both of you need to return to Him and to reach your divine potential.

Rather than be overwhelmed with all the things you think you should do or change, ponder and listen to the Spirit. It will tell you what you need to work on first. It will help you understand those things that apply just to you and just to your husband and how to use them to bless your marriage. Don't just say, "Well, the book said I should do this first." Instead, listen to the promptings of the Spirit and meditate on them. You will be guided to act on the things that you need to apply.

How to improve as a wife may not be something we usually ponder or pray about. This whole book is geared to helping you do just that. It is designed to help you carefully and clearly look at one of your most important roles. As you make your performance as a wife a matter of prayer, you will receive answers and direction. I think that often the Lord is just waiting for us to ask. So as important as I believe these concepts are, I believe that it is even more important to trigger those questions for you to ask the Lord. If I've done that, then all is well.

I know that there are some reading this book who are in very desperate circumstances, perhaps even abusive relationships, and may even be contemplating divorce. I hope and pray that some of the things we talk about will help you. If you need professional counseling, by all means get it! Even if your husband won't go. If you need that help, be brave enough to go get it.

Do know this: My prayers and love—and I trust those of many women reading this book—are with you. We know you're hurting. We pray the Lord will help you through this difficult time. Marriage is challenging, and there is much evil in the world. Have the courage—and the backbone—to protect yourself and your children.

But all of us can take steps to improve as a wife. The first one is to have confidence in this role. Just by your making the effort to learn more, you've already begun. So let's get started and work on this together.

NOTE

1. Quoted in Dell Van Orden, "Pres. Hinckley Notes His 85th Birthday, Reminisces about Life," *Church News,* 24 June 1995, 6.

CHAPTER 2

The Five Don'ts of Wifehood

"Let thy soul delight in thy husband" (D&C 25:14). Isn't that a beautiful instruction? We each must let our soul find that closeness and connection we want so much with our husband—and only with him.

There are several skills and attitudes that can help us be better wives.

As I thought about these, I realized that they were very similar to the Ten Commandments. But then I got to "Thou shalt not kill," and I thought—whew! Better not use that! (Remember, strangling your husband is *not* an option.)

As we begin learning how to be great wives, there are five behaviors that are very detrimental and that we should avoid.

1. Don't put other people before him.

We know that we should not have any intimate partner other than our husband. But I'm not talking just about sexual intimacy. I'm talking about mental and emotional intimacy. We should not be primarily confiding in or giving our primary emotional allegiance to anyone else—not Mom or Dad or sister or best friend or child.

The Lord has commanded us to cleave unto our spouses and

none else (D&C 42:22). Of this commandment, President Spencer W. Kimball taught: "The words none else eliminate everyone and everything. The spouse then becomes preeminent in the life of the husband or wife, and neither social life nor occupational life nor political life nor any other interest nor person nor thing shall ever take precedence over the companion spouse." A husband or wife who places children, friends, careers, hobbies, or Church callings before the marital relationship is "in direct violation of the command: None else."[1]

I was speaking on this topic when Barbara (remember that I'm changing most of these names) came up to speak to me. "How can I do that?" she asked. "My husband won't talk to me. If I couldn't talk about these things with my best friend, who would I be able to talk to?"

I said, "You talk about your marriage with your friend?"

She said, "Of course, I talk to her about everything. We talk almost every day and if I didn't, I think I'd go crazy. Over the years my husband talks to me less and less."

"Well, of course," I responded. She looked at me, startled.

"Do you complain about your husband to your friend?" I asked. Barbara responded that she did—because she had to talk to someone about it. "And do you sometimes discuss your intimacy?" She blushed a bit and admitted that sometimes she did. "Well, how would you feel if your husband discussed how dissatisfied he was with you when he was out with his best friend?"

She was shocked and said, "Over my dead body!"

"And what if he talked about your sex life?" She was now horrified.

"Well, if I was your husband, I wouldn't talk to you either," I said. She was a bit taken aback by that. "Think about it," I said. "Your husband is a smart man, and he knows you go off and chat with your best friend all about him and all about your marriage. Do you think anyone would confide in you?"

It was the first time she realized that she had been placing her friend above her husband as her intimate partner. This sobered her a great deal. She knew she would feel betrayed if her husband were to do what she was doing, but she had justified herself for years.

"Well, what can I do about it?" she asked.

I replied, "Go to your husband and say, 'You know what? I have realized that I've been choosing my friendships over you, and that's dead wrong. I realize I've betrayed your trust and loyalty, and I am so very sorry. I want you to know that from now on you will be my confidant, and I will keep our relationship private. I hope that I can earn your trust again.'" Then I told her she would have to tell her friend that what they had been doing was wrong and that she would no longer play the game. I told her she had to keep her mouth shut for a long time to earn her husband's trust back.

Then she uttered some very sad words: "I'm not sure I can do that. That would be too hard."

Oh, how sad. She was not willing to make that effort for her eternal relationship. It would have been difficult for a while—perhaps for even a whole year. But in the eternal scheme of things, a year is nothing. And she would have put her husband and their intimate, deep relationship at the top of priorities and regained a deeply satisfying bond that she was destroying.

Roberta was a young wife in the first few years of her marriage. As we all know well, those first few years can be challenging. Roberta was figuring out that men were a whole lot different from her college roommates. And there were so many odd things that her husband did and that his family did. They were driving her crazy. And of course the normal adjustments to intimacy were also challenging, both emotionally and physically. So she turned to the person she was closest to in the whole world, her mom. And she cried and complained to her mother. Often.

When I discuss Roberta's story in my lectures, I can see many of the young wives blushing. And I know that most of them are calling their moms and crying on their shoulders.

An interesting thing happened. Roberta's husband made a comment one day as they were having a disagreement, "Are you going to go crying to your mother now?" Sobering words.

Luckily, Roberta was blessed with a wise mother. Her mother finally said to her, "I will not discuss personal things about your husband with you. You need to learn to work these out, and you can pray to the Lord for help. But you are not to come to me and tell me the details of your marriage. I will discuss principles with you if you don't understand them, and we can talk about how to apply them, but we will not be talking specifics." What a wise mom!

We must place our husbands as the top priority in our intimate relationships. We need to confide in them and ferociously protect their confidences as well. As our husbands feel safe in our loyalty and dedication, they will open up more as the years go by, and a deep union will be the result.

When I was a freshman at BYU, my best friend–roommate and I spent the night on the lawn of the Marriott Center so we would be first in line to hear the prophet speak. On that occasion (September 1976) President Spencer W. Kimball gave a powerful talk on the topic of oneness in marriage. He said, "This [cleaving unto a wife] means just as completely that 'thou shalt love thy husband with all thy heart and shall cleave unto him and none else.' Frequently, people continue to cleave unto their mothers and their fathers and their chums. . . . All intimacies should be kept in great secrecy and privacy from others. . . . To cleave does not mean merely to occupy the same home; it means to adhere closely, to stick together."[2] That states it so clearly. To ılop the oneness we all desire, we must place no earthly thing

⌐⌐ ore our husbands.

The Lord, in speaking to Emma Smith (and to all women, as he states in the last verse) says, "Let thy soul delight in thy husband" (D&C 25:14). Isn't that a beautiful instruction? We each must let our soul find that closeness and connection we want so much with our husband and only with him. This may take time as we work out the kinks in our relationships, but we must always strive to place him first in all our earthly relationships.

When my three older sisters were young girls, they learned this lesson firsthand. One day they were all out of control. My dad came home from work and could tell that my mother had had a particularly exasperating day. He marched my three sisters out of the house to the front sidewalk, lined them up, and chewed them out royally. "This is my wife!" he exclaimed. "And nobody makes my wife upset, not even you. Frankly, if it's a choice between you or Mom, she stays." The girls were all shocked into silence. And that day they learned that my daddy loved my momma more than anyone else on the planet. And they learned that marriage comes first, even before kids.

But even though this principle is true, it is even truer that we can strike a balance, so neither the marriage nor the children suffer.

Finding such a balance is particularly difficult for wives. Sometimes we don't make our hubbies our top priority. This is very, very common. We begin having babies, and that mother-child relationship becomes all-absorbing. Let's face it. Having a new baby takes almost all of our time and energy and certainly is draining on our emotional energies as well. And just as we begin to get all that worked out, and the baby gets to be a bit independent, we have another one—and the cycle begins anew.

But wives who are not very careful begin to lose something important. Many women begin to switch their mental and emotional allegiances and their primary love to their children. Do you find yourself saying things like, "Well, I put my children first in my life," "My children are the most important thing in the world to me," and other similar statements? Most women do.

But as important as our children are, our husbands are more important. Our first and primary love must be to our husbands. An interesting thing happens if you do this. You still have an overflowing love for your kids. But your kids are now feeling safe and secure because they know that Mom adores Dad and that all is right in the universe.

Parenting author John Rosemond states, "The marriage precedes the children and was meant to succeed them. . . . We have accepted into our vocabulary the phrases 'child-centered family' and 'democratic family' seeming not to realize that when a child is regarded as being central, or equal, to his parents' relationship, their relationship is in jeopardy."[3] In fact, many women bristle when I tell them that they should have their primary love for their husbands because they've grown so accustomed to the worldly admonition to "put your children first."

So how are you doing in this regard? Let's take a little quiz to see how you're faring:

Quiz: Are You Married to Your Husband or Your Kids?

True or False

- Do your children stay up past 9:00 or 9:30 P.M. in the main family area? (Or, if you have older teenagers, do you have separate places where they can go so you can have alone time?)
- Do you go out with your hubby, without kids, at least three times a month?
- Have you been gone overnight without your kids and with your husband within the past year?

- Think about the last time you bought your kids a treat—do you buy your hubby a treat just as often?
- Analyze your conversations with hubby when it's just the two of you—do you spend more than 50 percent of the time discussing the kids?

Each of these areas is telling to see if you are putting other things or relationships ahead of your husband.

You need time each day to be just a wife to your husband. This is difficult to do with the children swarming around demanding our attention. That is why it is crucial to require that time every day. "The importance of putting a child to bed is so daddies and mommies can be husbands and wives again. Bedtime is an exercise in learning how to separate the child from the marriage," comments John Rosemond.[4]

Lynne had several children and was not very strict about bedtimes. She liked to let the kids just hang around and have lots and lots of family time. It is no surprise that now her marriage is in terrible straits and that she has very little relationship left with her husband. He was relegated to the position of "just one of the kids" and never has been able to get back into primary position.

When our children were younger, this was not nearly as difficult. Frankly, by about 7:00 or 7:30 P.M., I was pretty much done with being a mom, and so we put the children to bed early. As the children have aged, however, we can no longer insist that they go to bed that early—although I sure tried! But I guess it is unreasonable to expect teenage boys to go to bed at 7:00 P.M. But we have been adamant on the 9:00 P.M. rule. At that time, we insist that they go to their rooms. "Husband and Wife Hour has begun!" we intone and boot them (ever-so-gently) out the door to their rooms.

Sometimes my older one wants to stay up later, but he heads

downstairs to the family room while we have alone-time in the playroom. Sometimes they protest and I say, "Well, we might just start kissing!" and they usually scurry out in disgust. In fact, one night my youngest was particularly resistant. It was summer and he had been trying to push the time later and later. We asked him a few times to leave and he kept hanging around. Finally, I turned to him and said, "I would like to be a wife to my husband now. I love him dearly and want some time alone with him. You have until the count of 5 until I start really being a loving wife! 5, 4, . . . " He ran screaming into the other room that he was going to be permanently psychologically damaged!

Having this adults-only time is a daily reinvigoration of the marriage relationship and allows us to shed our "mommy-ness" and go back to being purely a wife.

This is not always easy. For a couple of years, I taught early-morning seminary (such a lovely euphemism for "ridiculously and inhumanely early teenage Church time") and I loved it. But it made for one tired puppy at 9:00 P.M. And I know there are many young moms out there and many morning-types who are entering zombie mode right about that time. We think, "Oh great, I've taken care of kids all day and now I have to take care of my husband?" My dear sisters, you must discover the wonders of napping. Learn to nap when your children do. Learn to nap when they go to school. And get enough sleep so that you can still be sufficiently coherent at the end of the day to be able to have at least some intelligent conversation with your husband who needs you. Now some of you may be in a position where napping is impossible due to commitments to work or other things. I urge you to adjust your schedule so that you can get a full eight hours of sleep most nights. Sometimes this takes some catching up a bit on weekends. And I know you have schedules that are stretched to the max. But as you make this a top priority, you will find you have added strength and emotional reserves to deal with the demands on your life.

If a wife is not careful, she will gradually lose her wife-ness and get consumed by mother-ness. When I listen to Dr. Laura on the radio, I sometimes cringe when I hear everyone say, "I am my kids' mom." Now that's not a bad thing to say, but I always yell at the radio, "I am my husband's wife first!" Feel free to yell at the radio. It's rather therapeutic.

Ask yourself, "How much time in the week am I a wife?"

Why do I spend so much time on this issue? Because I have seen many marriages break up when the kids leave home. I am an estate-planning attorney by trade and I have seen too many marriages end in divorce after twenty or thirty years because when the kids left, there was no relationship left.

Such was the case with Doreen. Doreen had a son and a daughter and was a devoted mother. Her husband was a devoted father. They spent hours and hours supporting and parenting their children—driving to and fro for every sport event, dance event, school event, and anything else they could cram into their schedule for their kids. Weekends were jam-packed—certainly no time left for a date with each other. Conversation centered around what the children were doing or going to do. And finally, the kids grew up and left home. And Doreen's husband looked across the table at her and realized he had no relationship with her at all. And he left. In fact, in that year, I had four different clients who had their marriages end: after twenty-one years, twenty-three years, twenty-two years, and thirty-five years. And each one was for the same reason: no kids = no relationship.

So ask yourself, are you starving your marriage to death?

Have you put other relationships before your husband? Remember the first Don't of Wifehood: Don't put anyone before your husband. Keep your most personal, your deepest, your most intimate self only for your husband and your marriage relationship.

In marriage, we give ourselves to our husbands. That means we give them our whole heart. We don't give that to anyone else.

2. Don't put other things before him either!

This is very similar to the previous rule, but it focuses on things. Ancient Israel was warned to have no graven images because that would shift their focus away from the Lord. Similarly, we must not shift our focus away from our husbands. Do not put money, house, job, or stuff before him or to replace him.

Now you may feel pretty safe on this one, so let's see how you're doing.

The Lord counseled women quite clearly on this topic. He said in Doctrine and Covenants 25:10, "Thou shalt lay aside the things of this world, and seek for the things of a better." He is very specific that women should not be obsessed with worldly things or desires. Obviously, seeking for "the things of a better" would include an exalted, eternal relationship with our husbands.

"Too many who come to marriage have been coddled and spoiled and somehow led to feel that everything must be precisely right at all times, that life is a series of entertainments, that appetites are to be satisfied without regard to principle. How tragic the consequences of such hollow and unreasonable thinking!" says President Hinckley.[5]

I remember a friend who sold Amway. As is common with these types of ventures, she was focused on acquiring things. She had a picture of a gorgeous mansion on her refrigerator. She and her husband lived in a small, humble home. I have to admit, that picture bothered me. I wondered how it felt to look at that picture day after day. It was a constant message to her husband:

"Man, you're a loser. I'm living in this hovel when I deserve to be living in a mansion!"

Now fast-forward ten years. Her husband is going through a terrible time of self-doubt, rebellion, and marital strife. I'm not saying that's all because of a picture on the fridge, but I do think that her fixation on "things" put undue pressure on her husband that warped their marriage relationship.

A great gift we can give our husbands is to be content and not make stuff more important than them. We can focus on living modestly and being appreciative of the life they provide us. That has to be a constant choice we make, because in this day and age we are bombarded with advertising and marketing to make us think we need more and better. It is difficult to stroll through a mall and not feel that pull of desire for more and more things. That's why I avoid the mall altogether! If you don't see it, you won't want it. (I once went to the mall for a post-Christmas sale and took my two youngest sons, who were seven and nine at the time. They walked in the mall and looked up at the magnificent Christmas decorations and said, "What is this place? Is this a palace or something?" I chuckled until I realized that they were dead serious. I said, "This is a mall, haven't you been here before?" Then I realized that I had never taken them there!)

Elder Joe J. Christensen counseled: "Some of the most difficult challenges in marriage arise in the area of finances. 'The American Bar Association . . . indicated that 89 percent of all divorces could be traced to quarrels and accusations over money' (*Ensign,* July 1975, p. 72). Be willing to postpone or forgo some purchases in order to stay within your budget. Pay your tithing first and avoid debt insofar as possible. Remember that spending fifty dollars a month less than you receive equals happiness and spending fifty more equals misery. The time may have come to get out the scissors, your credit cards, and perform what Elder

[Jeffrey R.] Holland called some 'plastic surgery' (*Ensign,* June 1986, p. 30)."[6]

If you need help handling your desire for graven images (aka Christian Dior, Tommy Hilfiger, Liz Claiborne, and so forth), I will share with you what helps me. One of the charitable ventures I'm involved in is Mothers Without Borders. We do international orphanage work. I have heard and seen many heart-wrenching stories of the extreme conditions that millions of orphans live in throughout the world. Not a night goes by when I do not utter a small prayer of gratitude for my bed and my pillow and my blanket. One of the projects we did was to make dresses out of T-shirts, which we sent to Africa. In the orphanage, they lined up all the little girls and had them count how many holes they had in their clothes. If they had ten holes or more, they got a new dress. Needless to say, after we heard that, we began sewing again and made several hundred more to send to the other girls. Most of the children had no blanket to sleep on.

Now think of that and go look in your closet. And tell me how you're struggling and feeling deprived. Walk through your house with the eyes of an orphan. We live in opulence.

Every day you can express gratitude to your husband for what you have. What a great message to our husbands: "You're more important than this worldly stuff that surrounds us."

I think of my mother. She grew up in poverty. All her adult life she has lived providently and has always had a lovely home for our family. Dad provided a good living for the family—not rich, but not poor. She was very appreciative of my dad working to provide for the family and I never, ever heard her complain over some thing or other that she did not have. What a great attitude to have, and what a vote of confidence for her husband. Because of her attitude, my dad has always felt proud of how he did in his career and how he provided for us. What a stark contrast to the mansion on the refrigerator!

Another way a wife could put money before her husband and marriage is to choose to work outside the home to support a lifestyle rather than necessities. In a talk on marriage, President Kimball said, "Young wives are often demanding that all the luxuries formerly enjoyed in the prosperous homes of their successful fathers be continued in their own homes. Some of them are quite willing to help earn that lavish living by continuing employment after marriage. They consequently leave the home, where their duty lies."[7]

An acquaintance I'll call Sheila worked full-time in a very high-powered position that required long hours and travel. I was rather surprised because she had four children at home and lived in a big house with every toy known to man—"toys" as in motorcycles, boat, RV, and so forth. Over the years I would hear her make comments such as, "I have to work because my husband would never make enough to keep me in the lifestyle I want." Or "I would really like a bigger home so I'm hoping for this promotion." This when she already lived in one of the biggest homes in the ward.

As her children reached teenage years, they began to have serious problems. I asked her one day, "How do you reconcile the counsel of the prophet to stay home with our children versus your working full time?" I was very curious, because I have struggled with this myself and have only worked part time out of my home since I had children. That choice was a hard one for me because I knew I could make a lot of money and have way cool stuff.

Sheila said something that chilled me then and chills me now, "Well, . . . that's good counsel for other people, but I need to work. My children and my husband know that they come first."

I was thinking, "When do they come first? Between 7:30 P.M.

and 9:00 P.M.?" Needless to say, her choice has had a terrible impact on her children and her husband. But somehow, she has convinced herself that the lifestyle was of primary importance to her and turned a blind eye to the cost.

We can put money and stuff before our husbands in very subtle ways. It can show up in the amount of time we spend caring for things or shopping for things. It can also show up in our contentment level, in how we view our lives in general.

It can help to attend the temple and look at our lives with that eternal perspective. Then we can look at our husbands with 20/infinity vision and see how important they are to us eternally. Keeping that focus will not only bless our husbands, but it will bless us as well as we lay aside the things of the world and focus on the better.

3. Don't speak ill of him.

A husband's name and reputation are sacred things. Treating our husbands with respect and extending that respect to protecting their privacy are crucial to being a smart wife.

When I was a young wife, I had several friends with whom I would go out to lunch fairly regularly. And like many other women, I would spend part of that time ragging on my husband about this or that. This would go on and on each month, with all the women complaining about their husbands. After one such lunch, I told my husband what we had all been discussing and found myself repeating some of the criticisms I had made about him. I will never forget the look of hurt and betrayal in his eyes. He very quietly said, "Merrilee, I would never say anything like that about you to anyone." And I knew he spoke the truth.

From that day on, I vowed to bite my tongue. I have tried my very best to never speak ill of him. It's interesting the impact that has had. We moved and I now have new friends and we try to not husband-bash. What a refreshing change to hear women who by and large are complimentary of their husbands and speak highly of them.

Now I cringe when I hear women bashing their husbands. Yikes! I wonder how their husbands would feel. Think about it. How would you feel if he talked about you the way you talk about him?

This applies to the things we confide to our parents. I was newly married and freaking out (as most all newlywed women do!), and I called my mom to cry. My mom stopped me in my tracks and said, "Do not tell me bad things about your husband. The two of you will make up and work things out, and I will still be feeling mad at your husband. So I don't want to hear it. You go pray for help and the two of you work it out." What a blessing that was!

Elder Oscar Kirkham had a saying many years ago: "Your name is safe in our home."[8] What a wonderful principle. I admit that I have truly struggled with this—not just with my husband but with people in general. But think of what a tremendous gift that would be to your husband. Have the integrity to be able to say to him, "Your name is safe in our marriage."

When we make this declaration to our husbands and strive every single moment of every single day to honor it, we lay the foundation for a secure and stable marriage. When we are counseled to be faithful to our husbands, this does not just mean morally. I believe that it also means emotional and verbal faithfulness.

Kim confided in me, "I hate it when my mom talks about my dad. All she does is complain, complain, complain. They've been married a long time and all of us keep hoping that she'll just let it go, but she doesn't. She tries to stop but then gives in and starts up again. I tell her, 'Mom, please don't talk about Daddy this way. I love him and it hurts me to hear this.' I've tried walking away. She gets better for a while and then slips again. It's just this horrible habit she has. I've been so sick of this that when I married, I swore I would never complain about my husband, and I keep my mouth shut. I don't think women realize the damage they do when they give in to this bad habit."

Contrast Kim's mother to a young woman I met several years ago. She had been married about eight years, so the "honeymoon period" was past. But you would never know it to hear her talk. She would say, speaking of her husband, "I remember when I looked across the room and saw the most handsome man in the entire world." And she would smile that wonderful, love-sick smile. She would talk about how wonderful he was. Now he was just a normal guy. And she was an extremely intelligent woman—certainly not a dependent doormat. But she had figured out early in her marriage that sweet compliments did much more for her marriage than sour complaints.

What we are doing is allowing our husbands the privacy to change and improve. There are things that we used to do as wives months or years ago that we no longer do. We have changed. We have hopefully improved. By keeping quiet to others about our husband's failings, we allow him that space and that time to change and improve as well.

In effect, we are saying, "Oh, most handsome, suave, and awesome husband"—go ahead and have fun with this!—"I have faith in you that you will try your best to change and improve throughout our marriage. To protect you in that effort, I will not complain or criticize you to others." What a tremendous vote of confidence. It's an effort in having faith in your husband, and that is absolutely at the pure core of faithfulness.

The constant harping on husbands has almost become a favored pastime of women throughout the country. Just watch TV and note how husbands are portrayed—bumbling, stupid, insensitive, wimpy—and the list could go on. We have become brainwashed that bashing men is not only normal but it is acceptable and downright entertaining.

Unfortunately, all this negativity is destroying marriages and making for many horrible wives. We must strive daily to not participate in this. Heavenly Father would not be pleased. And, frankly, we would be outraged if the tables were turned and our husbands did the same thing.

Stop now. Choose to protect your husband. Promise yourself that never again will you speak ill of your husband—never again.

4. Don't glue yourself to your spouse, and don't work too hard, but learn to rest from your labors.

One of the difficulties in working out a new marriage relationship is the amount of time the spouses feel they should spend together. That takes some time to work out. Often, but not always, the wife wants to spend more time with the husband than he feels is necessary. Sometimes the husband wants to spend more time with the wife than she would like. This takes adjustment, compromise, and lots of communication.

This principle of resting from the labor of marriage is an important one. To be a smart wife, we need to give our husbands space and time off, and we also need to take our own.

John Gray, the author of *Men Are from Mars, Women Are from Venus*, calls this idea "Cave Time" for the husband. He says that we need to have respect and understanding for a man's rhythms. If your husband needs fifteen minutes to unwind when he gets home from work, give it to him! Let him go hide out in his cave for a while and decompress and transition between his work life and his home life.[9]

Now I can just hear some of you whining (or screaming)— "Well, what about me?" And I have to admit, after some very long days (stretching months and years and decades!), by the time my husband got home from work, I was ready to throw all four little boys at him and walk out the door! Sometimes it felt like it took everything I had to hang in there until he walked in the door and I could collapse. I understand your reaction. But hear me out. (And don't worry—I'll talk about your time shortly.)

What do you want? Do you want a husband who dreads coming home? Do you want a husband who doesn't even get a minute to transition before he's dumped on? Do you want a husband who wants to be a good dad but is completely drowned with problems, whining, nagging, and delayed enforcement issues (ah, you know what I mean—"Just wait until your father comes home!") the minute he walks in the door?

So what I am recommending is that we give him some time to unwind. Give him a brief, sweet greeting from you and the kids. (Notice the word "sweet"—this, for the ill-informed, is the opposite of the attacking, whining, complaining, nagging, negative, exhausted onslaught we might be tempted to spew forth.) What we will get as a result is a hubby who delights in walking in the door of his home. We will get a husband who has time to move from his "work" brain to his "home" brain and can then better handle the parenting needs. We will get a husband who appreciates the loving reaction he gets when he gets home.

So is it worth hanging in there for fifteen minutes longer? Is it worth biting your tongue for a while longer? Absolutely.

So what other "cave time" does your husband need? Perhaps he needs some time to himself on Saturday. It amazes me that some women expect their husbands to devote 100 percent of every moment off of work to the family or to the wife. He's not the Energizer Bunny! For my husband, a long motorcycle ride did wonders. So on Saturday afternoon, off he would go. And he would come home wonderfully rested and refreshed. My friend was stunned that I would "allow" (and in fact, support!) him to do that. She would say, "Man, I'd never let my husband do that. I've had those kids all week and it's his turn." Oh, really? So he gets no downtime? Again, what do you want? I, for one, want a happy husband.

Now do not imagine for one minute that I only recommend giving your husband space. You need it for yourself as well. The only way you can be an excellent wife is to have your own needs met.

So how do you do that? Well, think to yourself what energizes you. What helps you to rest? For each of us, it will be different. For me there is no contest. Taking a nap ranks as number 1. So I take naps often. Napping time is almost sacred to me. I've had meetings rescheduled, choir practice moved—you name it— to accommodate my napping. It's become a ward joke that you do not mess with my nap!

I also need book time. I read a lot, and the family has learned that that's important downtime for Mom.

My friends have different space needs. One enjoys shopping— a lot. (Luckily, her husband can accommodate her space needs financially!) Another enjoys running. Yet another enjoys cooking. (Yes, some people actually do.) So whatever your space requirements may be, work it in!

Another important element in "resting from your labor" of marriage is to have healthy friendships. I learned this the hard way. When I got married, I thought you were supposed to be glued together. Isn't that what a loving marriage is? No way. After we had been married for a few years, things were . . . challenging. (How about that for a nice euphemism!) So I (who love to consult experts) went to a psychologist. I unloaded my tale of woe. The man patiently listened to me and then asked a very important question, "Do you expect your husband to take care of every single emotional need you have?" I was caught up short. I thought for a while. Then I had to admit that no, I didn't expect that. Then he counseled me, "Then go start meeting your own emotional needs." Great advice.

Having healthy friendships can be a wonderful blessing to a marriage and an essential element of being a great wife. Let's face it: women need womanly companionship. Our girlfriends understand how we think, how we feel, what we're going through. They can help us cope, support us, encourage us. In short, they can help meet our emotional needs quite well.

So I have developed many close friends. And at least once a month, Diane, Sue, Libby, and I (we call ourselves the Ya-Ya's[10]) go out together to do something fun. And we were there for Sue, who went through breast cancer (and all wore tiaras to celebrate when her hair grew back in). They have been there for me through the periods of long-term unemployment, losing my dad, losing an election, winning my election, you name it. We've been there for Diane through health issues and hair issues. We're there for Libby from weddings to unemployment to son issues. How could a woman survive without dear girlfriends? I don't know how. Certainly, I could never be the wife I am today without their support.

And they listen to all the "woman" stuff I want to talk about. So one day I'm explaining something to Stevie. . . . I can't remember what it was, but I think it was rather—"womanly"— and he turns to me and says with a pained expression, "Uh, no offense, but isn't this something you can discuss with your girl-friends?" I stopped short. And then laughed. Ha! He was right!

Guys need guy-friends and girls need girl-friends. So go get some. It may take a while to build those friendships. You really only need a couple of them. But they are invaluable in filling out your needs as a woman and in relieving your husband from carrying the entire burden.

Now with that said, I'll repeat an earlier caution. Girlfriends are dear, dear loved ones. But do not, I repeat, do not make them your emotional intimate above your husband. And do not bash your husband in front of them or share private information. Keep that boundary line clear.

Finally, another way to rest from the marriage is to take field trips. So if your hubby wants to go on a fishing trip, encourage him! Smile brightly and say, "Have a great time!" Then get out all those chick-flicks and chick-books you want and eat the food he hates. (We have tuna casserole when Daddy's gone because he hates it and we like it.) If he wants to go diving with his buddies, encourage him. Guess what will happen. The guys will all get together and they'll begin to talk. "Man, you would not believe what I had to go through to get to go on this trip." "Yeah, my wife has a list a mile long for me to do penance when I get back." "Me too. She won't let me live this down for a year." And then your husband will pipe up, "Gee, my wife was thrilled. She really encouraged me to go. She never has a problem with it." All the other guys will stare at him with slack jaws. And they will all say the same thing, "Lucky!" And he will think, "Wow, yes I am. I have the best wife in the whole world."

My, my, my. That sounds pretty good, doesn't it. And you know that that is absolutely what would happen.

Linda Jacobson Eyre agrees, "One of my funnest things to do is to literally run away. It is an organized run that I call my Day Away. When I had six children under nine, I only did my Day Away once a year, but now I find I can run away a little more often. I used to go sit in my van for the day or visit the library if it was too cold. Now, with a little more money in hand, I've thought of more exciting places. I spend the day thinking about myself for a change. I write down things I think I need physically, spiritually, emotionally, mentally, and socially. . . . By the end of the 24 hours away, it never ceases to amaze me how much cuter the children have gotten. And Richard, who has usually been tending the children (although I've been known to hire a babysitter or exchange days with a friend) is so much more sympathetic to the dilemmas of my life! It's a miracle every time!"[11]

So what kind of wife do you want to be? The kind who whines and complains, "You're leaving me with the kids? When do I get a break? We don't have the money for you to go off. What about that big list of chores you've been neglecting? Nag, nag, nag, whine, whine, whine, blah, blah, blah." This wife ends up with a resentful, bitter husband. She ends up with a husband who is burned out.

Or do you want to be the kind who says, "Why don't you schedule a trip in the next few months? You've been working so hard. You could use a break. I know how much you love backpacking. Why don't you set that up?" This wife ends up with a loving, grateful husband. She ends up with a husband who comes back renewed and ready to show love to her and the children in an even greater way.

You can decide.

I chose the latter and it was a great blessing to our marriage. My friends, at first, couldn't understand how I could be supportive of my husband going off with the guys to have fun. But now they have seen the results and have been converted. It is rather amusing, however. One of the things my husband just dearly loves is Scouting. I mean, he *loves* Scouting. He has spent over four hundred nights in a tent! (His favorite Book of Mormon scripture is "My father dwelt in a tent.") So for all his many years of Scouting (he's up to about twenty now, including eleven straight as Scoutmaster), he has gone on monthly Scout outings. Well, now the kids are older (the youngest turned fourteen) and they don't go as much. But guess who is still going monthly? Yup, Steve. It's not even his calling or anything. I just know that he loves it and it's his "recharging" weekend. I tease him a bit now that he goes even without his sons, but I have no problem with it. I know what I'll get back. A happy camper.

Again, with that said, you get to also schedule your own field trips! Woo hoo! So go visit your mother by yourself. Go have a weekend with the girls. Go visit a spa. Whatever floats your boat.

The Ya-Ya's have discovered the wonderful blessing of field trips. We encourage our hubbies to go out and have theirs—which they do. And we schedule our field trips. We go to BYU Education Week every year—just us girls. What a blast! We talk our brains out, shop our brains out, learn our brains out, and have a ball! And guess what the husbands get back? (Okay, I heard you—*not* a big VISA bill!) They get back happy wives!

And when I get back to my husband, I usually say the same thing, "Man, are you a good husband!" He's cool with that.

Now we've discussed several principles here—giving our husbands "space," taking our own, developing friendships, and scheduling field trips—that are all helpful in taking a rest from our work as wives. I shall add a small caveat here. Be smart.

Giving your husband "space" at the end of the day does not mean he gets to sit on his backside for two hours while you slave away. Encouraging him to go on field trips does not mean he gets to take off a week every other month without you. Nor does it mean that you can just take off for long periods of time either. Just be smart about this.

Keep a balance of taking time off versus investing the time in. But have enough "off-time" so that you can come back energized and renewed and a better wife for it.

While we're talking about time and rest, here's a related principle: It is really important to respect the rhythms of each marital partner. Some of us are absolutely great in the morning—alert, ready to hit the day's work, energized. These types typically crash by about 7:00 or 8:00 P.M., and by 9:00 they are pretty worthless. Then there are others who are very slow to reach a level of functionality in the morning, but once they get going they are good to go late into the evening. You know which of these descriptions fits you and which one fits your husband. Learn to respect those rhythms. Learn to work with them and make them work for you.

I am a morning person. At about 5:00 A.M., my brain wakes up and starts to run at 100 miles an hour. By 9:00 P.M., my brain is a sodden mess. My husband, on the other hand, is a confirmed night owl. For years, this drove me crazy. I would bound out of bed and want to hit the to-do list with a frenzy. So I would begin rattling off at my hubby all the things that needed to be done that day—trying to energize the huge lump that was still in a coma-like state. And if he did not leap out of bed and get right to it, I was irritated. Consequently, I was pretty irritated most of the time because I can't remember him ever bounding out of bed— not even during the many earthquakes we have had living in California. After a time (oh, say, like five years), I gave up the battle.

But I was still irritated. It took about another five years to learn to work this difference to our advantage. (I did mention earlier that sometimes I'm a rather slow learner.) It finally occurred to me that there were advantages in being married to a night owl. The bedtime ritual with our kids drove me crazy. Unlike those sweet mothers who read to their children and had lovely late-night conversations, once the kids started staying up until about 8:00 P.M., I was crabby. But luckily, a light bulb went off after a while. Let him handle it! It's his best time of the day!

Hence, we now have a routine that works. I drive the kids to seminary, do the whole morning family-prayer, breakfast, ready-for-school, off-to-school routine. (For many years, we propped Daddy up in bed for family prayer. He would rouse enough to call on someone and say "amen." We were all so proud!) Then Daddy does the night-time drill—getting the kids ready for bed, winding down the homework, dealing with the whole beauty regimen (quite speedy with boys), and the going to bed. He also handles picking up from work, picking up from dances, waiting up after dates, and so forth.

It's worked great. I've had great conversations with the kids in the morning, and he has had wonderful conversations with them at night.

So quit fighting those rhythms. If he's a morning person, don't save those deep discussions for the night. Time things so that they work well for both of you. And don't try to resist your own rhythms. If you're a mess in the morning, just adjust to that and don't heap on expectations. Also, when it comes to intimacy, learn to respect rhythms and be clear about your own. Nighttime is not the only time. Thank goodness!

5. Don't kill what worked at the beginning of the marriage.

Ha! You thought I wasn't going to say "Don't kill"! Well, I am!

So often wives ignore all those things that worked well in the beginning of the marriage and then, after several years have gone by, are left wondering what happened.

I'll share the case of Sarah. Sarah had been married about four years. As we were chatting, I grew a little alarmed. She confided in me that she often didn't bother to get dressed during the day if she didn't have to go anywhere. If she did get dressed, she'd throw on a pair of sweats. She admitted that on hot days, sometimes her husband would come home and find her in just her underwear to keep cool. Oy! I have to admit I gave her quite the talking-to!

In the beginning of the marriage, and indeed throughout your courtship, you looked good. A lot! You knew that you would never attract a husband if you looked lousy. So you made an effort. You did your hair. You probably wore a little make-up. You thoughtfully picked out your outfits to make sure you looked sharp.

Guess what? Whether you've been married for one year, one decade, or sixty years, it's still important! You need to look good.

I will share with you Mom's Best Advice number 7 (from my smart mother), "He's surrounded by babes at work. He doesn't want to come home to a slug." Think about it. Wherever your husband is, he sees women who take care of themselves. They had to dress up to go to work. They look good. But he comes home to you. What does he find?

Now this is not to suggest for one second that there is any hint of problems with loyalty or fidelity. Your hubby may be 100 percent completely loyal to you and completely in love with you. But look at yourself honestly in the mirror. Do you like what you see? Does your hair look good? Is it clean and styled? Does your face look good? Do your teeth look nice? Have you dressed well? Would you feel good walking in the front door and seeing you?

Or are you like many of the homemakers I see in the grocery store: bad roots showing, hair thrown up in a ponytail, T-shirt and sweatpants on (usually wrinkled), no makeup, bad posture, and a scowl to top it off? I think, "Man, who would want to come home to that?"

I'm not saying that you have to be a fashion model. He married you, didn't he? (Well, okay, so my husband couldn't get the phone number of Christie Brinkley at the time.) But every single one of us can look our very best. Every morning try to dress as if you were trying to get a date from your hubby that day. It would change things, wouldn't it?

I'll be talking about this more later, but just remember: don't kill what worked at the beginning of the marriage. Looking good worked. It still works. Try it.

Another thing that worked well at the beginning of the

marriage was talking—a lot! You remember those long nights where you got to know each other's soul. Remember when you spent hours just listening to him? That still works.

Look at how you talk to your husband—or should I say talk *at* your husband? Do your conversations consist of discussing the children, the bills, the household chores, gossip about the neighborhood, your latest acne outbreak, and so forth? Would any of that have been discussed when you were dating? Oh, I don't think so. He would have run screaming from the room.

So try having conversations as if you were courting. Try talking about things that involve your brain. Try listening to him for a long time. Go deep once again. He'll wonder what in the world is going on, so you may have to try this in snippets here and there. Give it a try. It worked before. It'll work again. He'll be dazzled.

A young married woman, Shantal, approached me one time and was concerned that her marriage was boring and had lost its "zip." I asked her an important question: "What worked at the beginning of your marriage that caused you to fall in love?" She thought about it. She answered, "Well, we loved ballroom dancing. We did it all the time." And then I asked the fateful question, "When was the last time you went dancing?" She admitted that they really hadn't gone dancing since they got married. Aye carumba! "That's it!" I cried. "This weekend you need to go dancing!" They did and rekindled wonderful feelings of love for each other.

When you were dating and a young couple, you did things together that you enjoyed. Are you doing them now? I would encourage you to try. And it can be a little different if you've aged. My parents loved to dance but when they were in their eighties, going out to dance didn't really fit. So every morning, my dad would dance with my mom in the kitchen and tell her she was beautiful. After sixty years, it still worked.

One of the reasons this works so well is that memories come flooding back when you repeat those activities. And so will the feelings that went with them. Love is resurrected!

So what did you do? Did you like to hike? Put that baby in the backpack and out you go. Did you like to go to museums and have heady discussion on art history? Guess what, museums are still there! Did you like to take long walks? You can still do it! Did you love Star Trek movies? Have at it! It may take creativity, but it always works!

In your courtship and early marriage, I can bet that you complimented your husband a lot. Let's face it, honey attracts bears. And even if your husband is now big and hairy (to continue the bear analogy), you can still compliment him. Tell him he's brilliant! Tell him he's hot! (Or use an expression that's more natural to you.) He may be skinny and bald and he may laugh, but he still likes to hear it. Tell him he makes your mouth water. Tell him you love his eyes. Tell him he looks fantastic in that jacket or those jeans. Be sincere in this, of course, but also have fun.

Have you killed compliments in your marriage? Don't kill what worked! Bring it back!

It's like pouring water on a parched flower. Keep pouring the water and it will revive and bloom. Don't we all love to hear them? And do not say them expecting to hear a compliment in return. Let that go. For now, concentrate on watering your husband. Over time, after he's not quite so parched, he will begin to notice you more as well.

Also compliment him to other people. Word gets around. Don't you love to hear someone say, "Gee, I heard so-and-so say the nicest thing about you." Spread that good honey all over the place. It'll work wonders.

As you pay attention to this small detail you'll realize how little wives compliment husbands. It is such an easy thing and can have great results in your marriage. And if you revive this sweet and loving practice, how will that make him feel? You can only imagine. And frankly, how will it make you feel as well— both toward him and about yourself? Great! Easy to do—big results.

Another thing you did when you were catching this handsome, intelligent bachelor was to flirt. Flirting! Yup, it's not just for dating anymore. Bring it back! If you've killed it, administer CPR immediately.

Now you're wondering how in the world one goes about flirting with one's own husband. Same as before. No different. Just act like he's a hunka-hunka burning love and you want him to ask you out. Piece of cake.

So bat those eyelashes. Stare at him across the room. Walk over to him and nibble his ear and say, "Hey, hey, hot stuff!" And walk by, slowly. Lean over at the restaurant and say, "I find you irresistible. Are you available later on?"

I know, you're laughing over this and wondering just when you should squeeze this in between breastfeeding and wiping spit off your shoulder. Or you're wondering how a seventy-year-old woman with the ravages of gravity readily apparent could ever pull this off.

Trust me.

Every single wife out there can flirt. Just give it a try! Copy gooey stuff you see at the movies. Have fun.

He will not care that fifty years has gone by. That's his hottie nibbling his ear. The results will be the same.

Even if you laugh and giggle and feel silly, so what! Keep it up!

Another thing that worked well in the beginning of the marriage was that you spent time together—a lot! You hated to be apart. Is that still a part of your relationship?

Grace had been married for fourteen years. Her days were filled with running kids here and there, keeping up the house, working her part-time job, you name it. Her husband was equally busy with a demanding job, a demanding church calling, and civic commitments. Add in the three kids with their demanding schedules. What was the result? Ships passing in the night. Little wonder that they didn't have much of a real relationship left. When asked how much time she spent with her husband, she laughed. "Well, we do see each other at church!" Great.

Ask yourself, how much time do you devote to this, your most important eternal relationship? Has it been relegated to last place?

Maria, on the other hand, was very smart. She turned down many opportunities so she could preserve time with her husband. She also kept in check the amount of activities her children were involved in. And she was careful to go on dates with her husband, spend time in the evening with him, go on walks with him, and just really make it a priority. This was pretty impressive because Maria had seven kids! But she also had a very healthy marriage. She understood that spending lots of time together would keep the relationship deep, solid, and rewarding.

Finally, when you were courting, you continually fell in love. Remember coming home to your apartment after another date? You would swoon at the door and your little heart would beat pitter-pat, and you'd think, "Man, I am so in love with this guy!" And your roommates would laugh at you. Even after many decades of marriage, it still works. You can continually fall in love. Go on a date. Go away for the weekend. Go on a walk. You'll fall in love all over again. We'll be talking about this a whole lot later on so I'll leave it at that. It works. Don't forget it.

President Kimball said, "There must be continued courting and expressions of affection, kindness, and consideration to keep love alive and growing."[12]

All those things that worked in the beginning of the marriage will work now. So take the time to look good. Talk a lot. Go do the fun stuff you used to do. Compliment him. Flirt with him. Spend time with him. And enjoy falling in love all over again. It'll work. Don't kill it. Love can be resurrected. And you know how to do it.

NOTES

1. Spencer W. Kimball, *Teachings of Spencer W. Kimball*, ed. Edward L. Kimball (Salt Lake City: Deseret Book, 1982), 311.

2. Spencer W. Kimball, "Marriage and Divorce," *1976 Devotional Speeches of the Year* (Provo, Utah: Brigham Young University Press, 1977), 151, 152.

3. John Rosemond, *Parent Power!* (Kansas City, Mo.: Andrews & McMeel, 1990), 6.

4. Rosemond, *Parent Power!* 97.

5. Gordon B. Hinckley, "What God Hath Joined Together," *Ensign,* May 1991, 73.

6. Joe J. Christensen, "Marriage and the Great Plan of Happiness," *Ensign,* May 1995, 65–66.

7. Kimball, "Marriage and Divorce," 146.

8. As quoted in Spencer J. Condie, *In Perfect Balance* (Salt Lake City: Bookcraft, 1993), 193.

9. See John Gray, *Men Are from Mars, Women Are from Venus* (New York: HarperCollins, 1992), 28–29.

10. See Rebecca Wells, *Divine Secrets of the Ya-Ya Sisterhood* (New York: HarperCollins, 1996).

11. Linda J. Eyre, "Moms Just Need to Have Fun," in *An Emotional First Aid Kit for Mothers* (Salt Lake City: Bookcraft, 1997), 188.

12. Kimball, "Marriage and Divorce," 147.

CHAPTER 3

The Five Do's of Wifehood

*As you seek out Heavenly Father's divine blessings to
flow upon your husband, you will also be inspired to assist
in that process and be a blessing to your husband. You will
find that your loyalty and devotion to him will increase.*

O kay, enough of the negative stuff! Let's talk about the
good things you need to do to be smart wives. You've
seen some great wives out there, and most of them have
learned these important principles. Each of these ideas can help
you achieve greatness in "wife-ness" if you're willing to give
them a try.

1. Do honor your parents.

These principles are tracking quite nicely with those Ten
Commandments, aren't they. Amazing how they apply to being a
wife.

Now just how does a wife honor her parents in her marriage? One important way is to keep them *out* of your marriage
intimacy. President Kimball expressed this well: "You love them
more than ever; you cherish their counsel; you appreciate their
association; but you live your own lives."[1] Good advice from a
prophet.

As I discussed before, we need to honor our parents' privacy and our own. This requires a clear boundary between the two marriages. You should not confide private, marital things to your parents (and frankly, they should not discuss theirs with you!). Honor them by not burdening them with your petty complaints about your husband and your marriage. Respect them enough to keep quiet.

There is one exception to this rule: if you are the victim of abuse in your marriage, talk to your parents immediately. You need their support if you decide you need to extricate yourself (and your children, if you have them). But absent this serious situation, you should keep quiet.

Matthew O. Richardson discusses separating from parents in his article "Three Principles of Marriage": "The first step in obtaining the heavenly form of marriage is for a man to 'leave his father and his mother.' President Spencer W. Kimball . . . taught that 'couples do well to immediately find their own home, separate and apart from that of the in-laws on either side' (*Teachings of Spencer W. Kimball*, 304). . . .

"This necessary step should in no way be interpreted as abandoning one's parents and family. While leaving established surroundings and relationships can be difficult and painful, it is necessary and serves a greater overall need. In fact, leaving has always been part of Heavenly Father's plan. Consider our premortal existence, for example. . . . God's requirement for us to leave His presence did not diminish His love for us, nor did it diminish our love for Him. In truth, this act accentuated the deep bonds of our love. Leaving the premortal estate was necessary for our development and growth.

"As we understand this concept better, we begin to see that we must leave more than father and mother. We might need to leave the familiar patterns of former friendships and sharing personal feelings with those who were once our confidants. Some married individuals have never left the single lifestyle to which they became accustomed before marriage. As a result, they are unable to enjoy the depth of a marriage relationship that otherwise might have been theirs. All couples can review their relationships, regardless of how long they have been married, to see if they have left or are allowing others to leave appropriately. . . .

"Perhaps the best outcome of appropriately leaving is that it allows a couple to practice cleaving to one another. . . . By scriptural definition, then, we find that God expects us to 'cling' to our spouse or to 'stick' with him or her. But it should also be understood that this is not a one-time event but a condition that lasts throughout a couple's marriage."[2]

Another way to honor our parents is to emulate what worked well. I was advised to do this in a blessing. At the time, I was all full of the hot and bother of being a teenager and thought, "Yeah, right, over my dead body!" But as I grew older, this was valued advice. What did your mother do as a wife that was good and helpful? Copy her!

My mom always looked good. She always took special care to keep her weight down and her clothes attractive. I have copied that as well. She went out with Daddy a lot. This we do as well. She was intelligent and strong and stood her ground. (Oy—all four daughters have copied that and are a frighteningly strong group of women!) The list goes on.

One day my youngest son approached me. He was all of about nine or ten. He said, quite seriously, "How am I supposed to learn how to be a good husband and daddy?" (No lie, rather obsessive child. Can't imagine where he got that from . . .)

I smiled and said, "Honey, you're in training right now."

"What? I am not!" he protested.

"Sure you are," I said. "Tell me all the things Daddy does to be a good husband."

He began, "Well, he takes you out on dates every week."

"Yes," I said. "And what else?"

"Well, he tells you that you look skinny!" and then he giggled.

I assured him that that worked well every single time. And away he went, listing all the things my husband did to be a great husband. He giggled contentedly and acknowledged that he was in fact being trained rather well!

So look at your parents' marriage and copy what worked well. I daresay you're probably already doing some of it (and saying, "Sheesh, I'm just like my mother!"). But if you're like me, I realized there was room for improvement. My mom always had dinner on the table at 6:00 P.M. when my dad got home from work. Let's just say I have been less than stellar in that regard. I have had to recommit myself to that one more than once. But it works. Now if I can just master that . . .

I have watched my nieces closely emulate my sister in their marriages. It's rather dear to see them make the same special foods, decorate their houses like crazy for the holidays, go on date nights, and on and on. I see them copying their mom in so many ways, and it is a blessing to their marriages.

A facet of honoring what worked in your parents' marriage is to be aware of how that marriage has influenced your own. So often we just go through our marriages on auto-pilot that we don't stop to see how our past experiences in the home of our parents are affecting us.

Author Rex A. Skidmore tells this story: "Jim and Carol had been married three months. . . . One Saturday at noon, when Jim returned home from four hours of classwork, he entered the apartment thinking of food and found none—only a note saying: 'Come see me, sweetheart. I'm downstairs doing the washing.'

"He sauntered downstairs. When his wife spotted him, she said casually, 'Honey, why don't you help me finish the washing?

Then we'll go upstairs and fix lunch together.' The sparks flew. He retorted that there was no way he would help with the washing. She became upset and he left. Why had trouble developed over such a circumstance?

"After awhile Jim returned and they talked through the whole situation. They then realized Carol had grown up in a home where her father often did the entire washing; Jim had been reared in a family where the mother would have run the father out of the house if he had even offered to help with the washing. When the differences in expectations were recognized, a compromise was made and a solution satisfactorily worked out."[3]

I remember the time my oldest son lost his first tooth. When it was loose, I told him to go see his father to help him pull it out. He went to his dad and his dad told him to go see his mother. After repeating this cycle for a while, I went to talk to my husband. "Why don't you pull his tooth out?" "Euuw, I don't want to do that!" he replied. "Besides, moms always do that." In my house, my dad always did that. In his house his dad was gone a lot driving truck, and so his mom did it. Frankly, neither one of us wanted to do it, so we compromised and told our children they could pull out their own teeth!

As we honor our parents and all that they taught us, we need to bring an awareness and an understanding heart to be willing to modify those practices to fit our own marriage. Just because "My dad always did that" or "My mother never did that" doesn't mean it always has to be that way in your marriage. Work through all these things you learned from your parents and keep the good ones and discard the ones that don't work for you.

We kept the "Dad does the dishes if Mom cooked" from my parents and modified it in our home to be "He who cooks does not have to do dishes." That worked for us and took the best from our families. We totally discarded "Dad never cooks" from *both* of our parents' families and added "All members of the family must take their turn cooking for the mutual survival of the family members." We kept the "Mom and Dad go on a date every Friday" from my family. We also kept "Mom gets to shop and no one complains" from his family. We totally abandoned "Mom controls the wash" in favor of "Mom does a lot of the washing but is assisted by all family members." We kept "Families were meant to spend a lot of time camping" but gave up "and Mom does all the cooking" in favor of "Mom does all the shopping but Dad does all the cooking because Mom purposely plays dumb on how to operate the camp stove." (Dang, just gave myself away!)

So when differences come up, look closely to see if these are just expectations that you've carried over from the way you were brought up. Honor the good stuff you brought and feel free to abandon the rest.

Another aspect of this is to honor your husband as the father of your children. Show him respect and appreciation for what he does as a daddy more than just once a year. I learned this from my friend Eileen, who was also raising four sons. She commented that it was important to her in the raising of four future fathers that she show great love and respect for her husband as their father. I have never forgotten that.

So I'm sitting in the car with the kids waiting for my husband to get in the car for church. Out he comes. And I gush, "You have the best dad in the whole universe!" The kids don't always react to that with glee and mutual appreciation (especially now that they're teenagers and in the obligatory "I hate anything parental" phase). But for their entire lives, I have raved about their dad as a great father.

This has different elements. Remember that he will handle things differently than you. The kids know that, so don't worry about it. Find things to compliment about his parenting and say them in front of the kids or your mother or strangers. Honor his fatherhood. The results will be excellent.

2. Do value him—don't covet another.

You've all met them. Those wives who are still pining away for what they didn't get—the ones who talk about their wonderful old boyfriends or ex-fiances. The ones who keep up a friendship or relationship with a male friend from before their marriage.

Coveting another is dangerous ground. President Hinckley says, "When you are married, be fiercely loyal one to another."[4] Being loyal to your husband is crucial to the relationship.

Wives can covet others by either wistfully thinking of prior flames or by comparing their spouses to other men and constantly finding them wanting. Both are disloyal. Both are dangerous. And both make for a lousy wife.

Really, what good does it do? How does it help? All it does is make you miserable and messes with your head.

Instead, we need to all work on valuing our husbands—focusing on the good that we *do* have.

Think about it for a minute. How would you feel if he sat there at the beach and looked at the women in bikinis? You'd feel terrible! He wouldn't have to say a word and you would *still* feel terrible. And you would be ready to do great bodily harm to him.

It is no different for a wife. When a wife does not fully value her hubby but instead covets others' behaviors, attributes, and so forth, *he knows it*. It is emotional betrayal.

The following story is a good illustration of the importance of valuing your spouse: "At one point in his marriage, Fred felt left out and unimportant. It seemed that all of his wife Janine's time and energy were consumed in serving their young children.

'I didn't know where I fit,' Fred says. 'It felt like I was only good for a paycheck.'

"Janine found that it took some planning to help her husband feel loved and valued. She decided that instead of a quick 'Hi, gotta run Molly to piano, bye,' when Fred came home from work, she would greet him with a smile, a tender kiss, and a comment like 'Now my day has started again. I'm so glad you're home.' Taking time away from other chores to lovingly greet her husband worked. Soon Janine found that sometimes Fred would see her at the stove, kiss her, and say, 'Now *my* day has started again.' Expressions of love like these help bring order to chaos and balance into life."[5] These expressions showed how much she valued her husband.

Remember that in the scriptures the Lord condemns the man who only lusts in his heart over another woman—even though he doesn't act on it. It is the same for us. We must not covet what we do not have. We must be mentally and emotionally *faithful*.

The Lord realized that the first steps to infidelity are mental. The first steps to sin are thought. And He taught His followers to nip themselves in the bud at that level—the mental level—and to stop the path of sin immediately.

You may feel very secure in your marriage and think that there is no way you would ever leave your husband or commit a sin of immorality. And that may all be true. But allowing these thoughts are still extraordinarily damaging.

Instead, focus on the good. Get out a piece of paper and a pen. Write at the top "Great Things about My Husband." Now start to write a list. Write down the way he holds your hand. Write down how he has cute feet. (Don't laugh, my hubby has the cutest feet!) Write down that he took care of the whole house when you came down with the stomach flu. Write down how he loves snuggling your babies. Write down how he took care of your dying father so sweetly. Write down how he looked across the altar when you were married. Write down how he wrote you that cute love poem you have hanging above your desk. Write down how he didn't complain when you wanted to paint the family room red. Write down how he baptized your children, and gave you a blessing, and danced with you, and walked with you, and told you he loved you.

Okay, I don't know about you but I'm a weeping mess right now. Just keep writing. Spend an hour on it. Or more.

Now go in and look at your husband. How do you feel about him now? Couldn't stop yourself, could you? You went over and kissed him, didn't you? See.

Value your husband. Value him deeply. In fact, get a "Why I Love My Husband" book and write down every day some little thing that's wonderful about him or something nice he did. It will transform your marriage. It will transform you.

Dr. Victor B. Cline, in discussing what every husband wants from his wife, states the following:

"[Here is] what, in my judgment, most husbands really want. . . . Fill his cup, and he will be yours forever.

" . . . *Accept and approve the husband.* I cannot overemphasize the importance of this. Most husbands are out there every day fighting the dragons, and when they come home at night they want their wives to be proud of them, appreciate their contributions and sacrifices, believe in them—be on their side. The loving, understanding wife is the husband's shelter in the storm. She should be the one who patches up bruises, nurtures him, and heals and builds his battered ego, and sees and treats him as a prince in their kingdom. He needs to understand that he is number one in her life above all other people."[6]

So when those snaggly little thoughts of criticism or complaint come to your mind, stop yourself immediately. Take a deep breath. And then quickly fill your mind with some of the sweet things from your list. It will banish those dark thoughts from your mind and give you a better perspective to deal with the differences that are there.

You may feel that everyone else's husband is so much better than your own. Stop that right now. Go buy your little book. Begin today. Appreciate the little tiny things. And over time, you will value your husband so much you will wonder how in the world you could have ever felt differently.

Do value him.

3. *Do value yourself.*

Now while you're at it, you need to value yourself as well. A perfect wife understands how important it is to value herself so she can be her very best.

President Hinckley counseled: "Well, you dear women, I say thanks to you. Thank you for being the kind of people you are and doing the things you do. May the blessings of heaven rest upon you. May your prayers be answered and your hopes and dreams become realities.

"You serve so well in the Church. You think it is so demanding. It is. But with every responsibility fulfilled, there comes a great reward.

"Many of you think you are failures. You feel you cannot do well, that with all of your effort it is not sufficient.

"We all feel that way. I feel that way as I speak to you tonight. I long for, I pray for the power and the capacity to lift you, to inspire you, to thank you, to praise you, and to bring a measure of gladness into your hearts.

"We all worry about our performance. We all wish we could do better. But unfortunately we do not realize, we do not often see the results that come of what we do. . . .

"Now, my dear sisters, that is the way with you. You are doing the best you can, and that best results in good to yourself and to others. Do not nag yourself with a sense of failure. Get on your knees and ask for the blessings of the Lord; then stand on your feet and do what you are asked to do. Then leave the matter in the hands of the Lord. You will discover that you have accomplished something beyond price. . . .

"You know as I do that God our Eternal Father lives. He loves you. You know as I do that Jesus is the Christ, His immortal Son, our Redeemer. You know that the gospel is true and that heaven is near if we will cultivate it in our lives.

"You are the Relief Society of The Church of Jesus Christ of Latter-day Saints. There is no other organization to equal it. Walk with pride. Hold your heads up. Work with diligence. Do whatever the Church asks you to do. Pray with faith. You may never know how much good you accomplish. Someone's life will be blessed by your effort."[7] Wonderful counsel from our prophet, and all of it is geared to helping us recognize our value and our worth. He understands our value, and so does our Heavenly Father. It is important that we come to that understanding as well.

In your marriage, you must choose to be a partner in the marriage relationship—not a limited partner, not the general partner, but a full and active equal partner. Let's do a little math experiment to see how this works.

What is one times one? That's right. It equals one! (Although when I talk about this in a lecture, someone invariably calls out "Two!") One full partner with one full partner equals true oneness in the marriage. Now, what is one times zero? Yup. It equals zero. So what does this mean? It means if you treat yourself as a big fat zero in the relationship, nothing good will be the result.

This is the Doormat Principle. If a spouse (usually the wife) chooses to be a doormat—that big fat zero—the relationship will be a big fat zero as well. Do not be a doormat spouse! Do not be a dependent, apologetic, weak-willed nonpartner. This is crucial for a wife. Men do not feel good about themselves when you let them be overly controlling. And they have no respect for you. A good relationship cannot result.

On the other hand, you will have respect when you take care of yourself and respect yourself. If you take the time to develop yourself as a full partner, then you can have the true oneness in marriage that you so desire.

The best wife is a *true* person. She develops her own unique gifts and abilities and is constantly evolving and growing. In an *Ensign* article many years ago, Ann Reese stated, "There are within each woman certain unique qualities—her intelligence, her combination of talents and positive personality traits, her inner self, her soul—which are of immense worth. It is the duty of each woman to come to know and accept and enjoy being herself. She must respect her own inner strengths and from this self-acceptance be secure enough to live courageously and righteously and to reach out in service to her family and fellow beings."[8]

If we make the effort to truly value ourselves, nothing can stand in the way of our developing into not only a great wife but a great woman as well. One of the great mistakes wives make is to *stop growing*. They tend to mistakenly conclude that they snagged their man and can now coast to the celestial kingdom. Actually, that wedding is only the very first baby step in a series of steps that will lead you there. Now is not the time to sit down. It is the time to value yourself.

We'll be discussing this in great detail in the next chapter. I bet you can't wait!

4. Do gain an understanding of what a man is.

Understanding men is really helpful to your marriage relationship. I must admit that I had to work on this one. I am the fourth daughter and had only one brother. I wasn't quite up to speed on guy-ness when I got married. (Of course the Lord, with his inimitable sense of humor, sent me four sons. I had to learn fast!)

As we study "maleness," we learn that our perspectives are different. They look at the world differently than we do. But it's just like glasses are different for each person. Is one right and the other wrong? No, each perspective is just different and suited to our needs and circumstances.

One of the biggest insights gained in my marriage is that my husband thinks like a guy. Wow! What a revelation! Often when he wasn't talking, it was because he didn't have any deep thoughts to share. Nothing personal.

So I had to learn about how my husband thinks. He's pretty linear and uncomplicated in his thinking. He doesn't analyze every relationship and every conversation ad nauseam like I do. He doesn't care that much about what others think. He's pretty straightforward. Understanding all of this really helps me let go of all the little hurts, misunderstandings, and unrealistic expectations I might otherwise harbor.

Of course, men have their differences. But it can safely be said that men in general think differently than women do. In an article about Dr. Michael Gurian and his book, *What Could He Be Thinking: How a Man's Mind Really Works,* we read: "The male brain secretes less of the powerful primary bonding chemical oxytocin and less of the calming chemical serotonin than the female brain.

"So while women find emotional conversations a good way to chill out at the end of the day, the tired male brain needs to zone out all that touchy-feely chatter in order to relax—which is why he wants the remote control to zap through 'mindless' sport or action movies. [Actual proof that he needs to head to his cave for a bit when he gets home. . . . So it's not personal. Who knew?]

"His brain takes in less sensory detail than a woman's, so he doesn't see or even feel the dust and household mess in the same way. Anyhow, the male brain attaches less personal identity to the inside of a home and more to the workplace or the yard—which is why he doesn't get worked up about housework. [Aha, don't tell my husband this!]

"Male hormones such as testosterone and vasopressin set the male brain up to seek competitive, hierarchical groups in its constant quest to prove self-worth and identity. That is why men, paradoxically (from a hormonally altered new mother's point of view), become even more workaholic once they have kids, to whom they must also prove their worth.

"Gurian says his book is aimed mainly at women. 'Men get this already. They are living this brain but they don't have the conscious language to explain it. Women are not living it. . . .

" 'I beg people to go back to nature, look at the PET scans, look at the brain differences and see if it makes sense.'

"If it does, the consequences are profound for a generation of 'liberated' women brought up to believe it is men who have to change, and men who must respond to a female way of relating in order for marriage to succeed.

"Gurian says men can learn new skills and alter their behavior, but they will not be able to meet all of women's expectations.

" 'Popular culture focuses so much on trying to get people closer. Most people believe that marriages break up because men and women are not close enough. But what I am learning about the brain leads to the idea of intimate separateness, in which the brain seeks less intimacy at times,' Gurian said.

" 'People want to love each other. If we can learn who we might be—not what IS he thinking, but what COULD he be thinking—then I am optimistic.' "[9]

Interesting, isn't it? Just reading a bit helps so much in our understanding of these men we're married to.

The studies on the differences between male and female brains are fascinating. A BBC report on Science & Nature commented on the studies that have been done on the brain, "There is growing evidence that men and women's brains are wired differently. This theory may explain the finding that, on average, men are better at some things and women are better at others.

"For example, studies have found that women tend to be better at *empathising* and men are generally better at *systemising*. In other words, men are often more adept at discovering the rules that govern a system. They like to get deeply involved in activities such as car repair, computing or building up an extensive music collection.

"Women, on the other hand, are thought to be better at guessing other people's emotions and responding appropriately. They would be more likely to comfort you in a time of crisis."[10]

Another study at the University of California at Irvine stated, "In general, men have approximately 6.5 times the amount of gray matter related to general intelligence than women, and women have nearly ten times the amount of white matter related to intelligence than men. Gray matter represents information processing centers in the brain, and white matter represents the networking of—or connections between—these processing centers.

"This, according to Rex Jung, a UNM neuropsychologist and co-author of the study, may help to explain why men tend to excel in tasks requiring more local processing (like mathematics), while women tend to excel at integrating and assimilating information from distributed gray-matter regions in the brain, such as required for language facility.

"These two very different neurological pathways and activity centers, however, result in equivalent overall performance on broad measures of cognitive ability, such as those found on intelligence tests."[11]

Brent A. Barlow, a marriage expert, suggests that understanding these differences can help improve our marriages. He says, "Most married couples soon discover that differences arise in marriage simply because one is male and one is female. . . . In her book *What Every Woman Should Know About Men*, Dr. Joyce Brothers asked and answered this interesting question: 'Are men and women really so different? They are. They really are. I spent months talking to biologists, neurologists, geneticists, research psychiatrists, and psychologists. . . . What I discovered was that men are even more different from women than I had known. Their bodies are different and their minds are different. Men are different from the very composition of their blood to the way their brains develop, which means that they think and experience life differently from women.' . . .

"The basic facts couples should realize are that the differences between the sexes are real and that they must be taken into consideration in marriage."[12]

So pay attention. Learn about how guys work. It'll help you understand a bit more how he sees things and will help tone down reactions you might otherwise have.

Ask yourself, do you really want a wife? Or do you want a husband? Okay, honestly, I could use both. But I want my husband to be my husband and to be a man. That's why I married him.

As you can see, it is very helpful to study a bit, read a few articles, and be aware of the differences. As you begin to understand men better, you will also value your husband more. That's a great step in becoming a terrific wife.

5. *Do value your commitment.*

A dear friend said to me one day, "I want the same testimony of my marriage as I do of the Church." An interesting concept. I mulled that one over for a long time.

Another friend, in discussing this topic and looking forward to one of my lectures, said, "Oh good. Maybe I can learn to love my husband."

Clearly, there is a need to value our commitment in our marriage.

Let's be honest. All our marriages are at various levels of love and commitment. Even within our own marriage, my husband and I have varying degrees from year to year. Hopefully, we can work on improving our present feelings and move them in a positive direction.

In "The Family: A Proclamation to the World" we read: "We, the First Presidency and the Council of the Twelve Apostles of The Church of Jesus Christ of Latter-day Saints, solemnly proclaim that marriage between a man and a woman is ordained of God and that the family is central to the Creator's plan for the eternal destiny of His children. . . .

"The family is ordained of God. Marriage between man and woman is essential to His eternal plan. . . . Successful marriages and families are established and maintained on principles of faith, prayer, repentance, forgiveness, respect, love, compassion, work, and wholesome recreational activities."[13] The seriousness and importance of our marriage cannot be taken lightly.

For most of us who got married in the temple, making the choice of whom to marry was a huge deal. We knew that this decision affected us eternally. So we did not make this decision lightly. Truthfully, it's a rare soul who makes the marriage decision lightly.

My courtship with my husband illustrated this. The prior year, I had gotten within five weeks of marrying another man. When that relationship fell apart, it was devastating. Needless to say, I was very gun-shy about relationships. So as Steve and I were dating and as things progressed, I would say, "Well, I think I love you a whole week's worth." After a while longer, I said,

"I'm pretty sure I love you a year's worth." And on it went. I had his wedding ring engraved with, "I love you an eternity." For me, that was huge.

As young couples move forward into the marriage relationship, they have many experiences that test this resolve and commitment. We have all had times when things were not that fantastic and we wondered, "Brother, are we even going to make it?" As an elderly friend of mine jokingly commented, "I never thought about divorcing him, but I thought about killing him several times!" My husband and I have each had experiences that made us wonder if this relationship had what it took to make it throughout the year, much less the eternities.

So how do I get that testimony of my marriage? A few things can help.

First, realize that it may take time. How long did it take for you to get a testimony of the Church, even if you were raised in it? It took time. You have an eternity. Give it time and patience and commitment. For some couples, it may take a decade, some a lifetime. Each will be different. But each one takes time.

Second, pray for your husband specifically and daily. This will add a level of commitment that you may not have had before. As you seek our Heavenly Father's divine blessings to flow upon your husband, you will be inspired to assist in that process and be a blessing to your husband. You will find that your loyalty and devotion to him will increase.

Third, ask your Heavenly Father for this testimony. Again, be patient with the answer. It took me a long time to get there. It had absolutely nothing to do with my husband and everything to do with me. So ask Heavenly Father for this blessing, and then patiently go through the lessons and experiences He'll place in your life to get you where you need to be to receive it.

Finally, go do sealings in the temple and listen to the promises and blessings. Also, do initiatories to hear your blessings in your own capacity as a wife. These will help you see the eternal importance and value of your eternal relationship. Understanding and love and commitment will distill upon your soul as you do this.

Personally, it took me twenty years to get this testimony. As I mentioned, it had everything to do with me. While I was growing up I saw several family members go through many divorces. Needless to say, I was extremely apprehensive and worried that my own marriage would not be able to survive. I'll never forget our fourteenth anniversary. In fact, I remember exactly where we were sitting, eating chowder in bread bowls in Monterey, California. I looked deeply into my husband's eyes and said, "I have now realized that you will never leave me." He said, "No, I never will." And I knew that that was true. It was the first step in being able to trust and commit to a deeper level of relationship.

After many more experiences that I will discuss later, I finally received that testimony of my marriage. What a gift! The growth of love and commitment then really began to increase exponentially.

Now you may be a whole lot faster or you may be slower. What matters is that you are working on it and that you are valuing your commitment.

Realize that your husband is your eternal companion. Learn to look at him that way. Elder Lynn G. Robbins sums this up: "Scripturally, the Lord is very clear with us on this doctrine— you can't 'fall out of love,' because love is something you decide. Agency plays a fundamental role in our relationships with one another. This being true, we must make the conscious decision that we will love our spouse and family with all our heart, soul, and mind; that we will build, not 'fall into,' strong, loving marriages and families. 'Don't just pray to marry the one you love. *Instead, pray to love the one you marry*' (Spencer W. Kimball, quoted in Joe J. Christensen, "Marriage and the Great

Plan of Happiness," *Ensign,* May 1995, 64; emphasis in original).

"Let us hearken to President Hinckley's counsel: 'I lift a warning voice to our people. We have moved too far toward the mainstream of society in this matter. Now, of course, there are good families. There are good families everywhere. But there are too many who are in trouble. This is a malady with a cure. The prescription is simple and wonderfully effective. *It is love.* It is plain, simple, everyday love and respect. It is a tender plant that needs nurturing. But it is worth all of the effort we can put into it.'"[14]

It is only by a constant, committed effort that we will make the love we share with our spouse a constant for eternity.

Several years ago, I witnessed true love. I will never forget it. I was attending the dedication of the Detroit Michigan Temple. I had grown up there and had gone back to see my mom put her book, *The Michigan Mormons,* in the cornerstone and to see the dedication. President Hinckley began speaking. He was discussing various things, as he sometimes does. Then he began to talk about eternal things. And then he paused and said, "You know, this morning I sat across from my wife at the breakfast table and I looked at her hands. They are wrinkled and gnarled with age. And I thought, these are the most beautiful hands in the world." He paused and was emotional for a long time. Then he continued, "Oh, how I love my wife. She is everything to me."

I will never forget witnessing true love and commitment. I saw there a devotion that ran deep and wide and for all eternity.

I witnessed that kind of true love again two years ago. My dear daddy was dying. He and Momma had been married for sixty-one years. They had stuck together through wars, five kids, unbelievable heartaches, trips throughout the world, the joy of seventeen grandchildren, and growing old. Now it was time for Daddy to go. I watched the tender ministrations of my mother. I saw the devotion and sweet, sweet love that poured from her soul. And I watched her tenderly kiss him good-bye for a time. True love. Commitment.

It is my abiding hope that I can be that kind of wife to my husband—that when we've been married for many, many decades, he will feel that kind of love for me and I for him.

NOTES

1. Spencer W. Kimball, "Marriage and Divorce," *1976 Devotional Speeches of the Year* (Provo, Utah: Brigham Young University Press, 1977), 152.

2. Matthew O. Richardson, "Three Principles of Marriage," *Ensign,* April 2005, 20, 21, 22.

3. Rex A. Skidmore, *Marriage: Much More Than a Dream* (Salt Lake City: Deseret Book, 1979), 5.

4. Gordon B. Hinckley, *Teachings of Gordon B. Hinckley* (Salt Lake City: Deseret Book, 1997), 328.

5. Gary and Joy Lundberg, "The Marriage Balancing Act," *Ensign,* January 2000, 57–58; emphasis in original.

6. Victor B. Cline, *How to Make a Good Marriage Great,* rev. ed. (Salt Lake City: Bookcraft, 1996), 16.

7. Gordon B. Hinckley, "To the Women of the Church," *Ensign,* November 2003, 113, 114, 115.

8. Ann S. Reese, "Being a Wife," *Ensign,* September 1984, 58–59.

9. "Brain science reveals what men are really thinking," *Reuters* (October 2003); from http://www.michaelgurian.com/usa

10. "Brain Sex," emphasis in original; from http:/www.bbc.co.uk/science/humanbody/sex/articles/brain_sex.shtml

11. "Intelligence in men and women is a gray and white matter"; from http://today.uci.edu/news/release_details.asp?key=1261

12. Brent A. Barlow, *Dealing with Differences in Marriage* (Salt Lake City: Deseret Book, 1993), 28, 29–30, 32.

13. "The Family: A Proclamation to the World," *Ensign,* November 1995, 102.

14. Lynn G. Robbins, "Agency and Love in Marriage," *Ensign,* October 2000, 22.

CHAPTER 4

How to Combine "He" and "She" and *Not* Lose the "Real Me"

*We must keep the Real Me alive and well-fed in order
to develop into who we were meant to be.*

Getting married is weird. You've spent twenty some-odd years figuring out who you are. Then you get married. So now you're a wife. What's that? How do you DO that? Are you still the same person? Should you change?

Think back to the day you got married. I remember it well. I remember the night before chatting with my sisters (who were full of good advice) and feeling excited and yet still . . . single. Then less than twenty-four hours later, I'm driving home from the temple with my husband thinking, "Whoa. I am a WIFE. I am Mrs. Boyack. . . . Now what?" I had never been a wife. I didn't know who the new "Mrs. Boyack" was—or should be. In fact, it took many years to get used to saying, "I'm his wife." Or answering to "Sister Boyack" or "Mrs. Boyack." One minute you're single; the next minute you're a wife. So strange.

Add all the expectations of your husband, all the expectations of your in-laws, all the expectations of your parents, all of *your* expectations, and then all the expectations of everyone around you—friends, Church, community, and so forth—and you can get pretty lost in the mix. In the midst of this, you may feel like crying out—Will the Real Me please stand up?

How do we combine "He" and "She" and still keep the "Real Me"?

After marriage, many wives are starving. I don't mean this in the literal sense. But I have discovered as I have spoken before literally hundreds and thousands of women that many, many wives are starving themselves emotionally, mentally, and otherwise. They get subsumed in caring for husband and children and in doing all the expected tasks of being a wife and mother. The consequence is that personal development and time for the wife gets pushed farther and farther back on the priority list.

The end result is a woman who is tired much of the time, unattractive much of the time, hasn't read a book in who knows when, and feels like a squirrel on a treadmill. Much of her zest for living has been zapped. The wife knows that this is not really who she wanted to be, but she is often too exhausted to do anything about it.

Take a minute now to think about yourself. Think back to when you were in your early twenties and so idealistic. Have your dreams for yourself come true? Is your life like you imagined? Do you look and act and feel like you thought you would?

I remember one day I was driving down the road and I turned to my teenage son and said, "Shoot me now!"

He thought that was a rather strange request and said, "Uh, okay. I sense you're having a problem?"

I explained. "When I was a young woman, I swore that I would never put on weight, I would never go around in a T-shirt and sweats, and I would never ever end up being a frumpy, dumpy housewife. Here I am in a T-shirt and sweats [I had been painting and had to stop to go drive carpool], I need to lose twenty pounds, and I'm driving a big honkin' van filled with smelly teenaged boys. I have become the frumpy, dumpy house-wife. Shoot me now, and put me out of my misery."

Luckily, this son was very kind and said, "Aw, Mom. Get a grip. You're not that bad." Strangely, that left-handed compliment helped.

Okay, I was just having a bad day that I chuckle about now. I'm sure you have those too. As I honestly evaluate my life, I'm grateful I'm a wife and mother and for the most part am very happy with how my life is. And there are things I still want to work on.

Truthfully, there is no way we could live up to the idealized image we had when we were young. But we can and should strive to improve and try to be the best we can be. It's when we give up that we begin to stagnate, and then hopelessness and drudgery set in.

Well, today is a new day! Today we can begin again to do something about our lives. Today we can resuscitate the "Real Me" that's lurking in there underneath those twenty extra pounds and sweatpants. . . . Okay, maybe *way* underneath—but it's there! Let's go find her.

Nourish Body, Mind, and Spirit

Elder Marion D. Hanks said, "Every girl, every woman, is a somebody, apart and aside from anyone else, husband or family or otherwise."[1]

We must keep the Real Me alive and well-fed in order to develop into who we were meant to be. I love how the scriptures define this. They use the term filling the "measure of [our] creation" (D&C 88:19). I often review my life to see if I am filling the measure of my own creation. Being a wife and a mom, as critical as they are, are only *parts* of this measure of creation—not the entire thing. We must feed each part, including being a wife and a mom. And the nice thing is that we don't have to fill every part equally at every time. But neither can we starve them all the time and expect to succeed.

Elder Hanks further said, "Self-respect and self-esteem are the products of good self-image."[2] It is working on that self-image that I want to talk about in detail. We worked on it a lot at some point in our lives, but often, as we work on the self-image of our children, our own work got shunted aside. But this work—this personal development—cannot take backstage.

President Gordon B. Hinckley said: "I have been quoted as saying, 'Do the best you can.' But I want to emphasize that it be the very best. We are too prone to be satisfied with mediocre performance. We are capable of doing so much better."[3]

We *are* capable of doing so much better. And it doesn't necessarily consist of having to do a whole lot more. It sometimes simply involves an awareness and priority shift to do things better, more efficiently, or perhaps just in order.

Let's talk about three aspects of nourishing the Real Me that is within you. They consist of nourishing your body, mind, and spirit. Since nourishing your body is probably the most problematic for many of us, I'll talk about it first.

Nourish Your Body

Once upon a time there was a beautiful young princess. She was sought after by all the charming princes in the surrounding castles, kingdoms, wards, and stakes. She was slim and fit and wore lovely princess clothing and wore lovely princess makeup and had lovely princess hair. Finally, she picked her favorite Prince Charming and he carried her off to his far kingdom and his castle. She was so very happy. She began to work on managing a castle, which was no small feat, let me tell you, and spent many hours cooking, cleaning, shopping, and so forth. (Alas, this was during the Fifth Kingdom when good help was *so* hard to come by.) Soon, little princelies and little princessettes were born to the happy family. Our fair maiden worked even harder, carting her royal lineage to local jousting practice, princessette training school, and so forth.

As things became busier, the lovely princess makeup was the first to go. Espousing a "natural" look (i.e., *raw*), our beautiful princess said, "Alas, I do not have time to put on gloss or blush and shall adopt a more earthen look." (Sadly, our beautiful princess had not clued in to the fact that most princes don't run around saying, "Gee, look at that hot princess. She's so *'earthy.'* Hubba-hubba!")

Next to go were the princess clothes. As our fair maiden had grown and changed, her clothes no longer fit her more queenly frame. She kept a few and kept attempting to squeeze her queenly frame into princess-frame clothing with some dubious success. (Although the entire kingdom is still mourning the tragic blinding of her faithful dressing-maid that occurred when a button popped off said princess's clothing and took out her poor dressing-maid's eye.) The princess just didn't have time to find any pretty queenly clothes and didn't really have a clue about how to dress more like a queen anyway. As time went on, the Kingdom T-shirt and the Kingdom-brand sweats grew more appealing (and one can be sure that at least no servants were lost or injured in the wearing of such apparel).

The princess's hair had changed dramatically over time as well. The princess was far too busy and far too cheap to visit the Royal Hairdresser to have her roots managed, and once again succumbed to the "earthen" look, i.e., drab, graying roots followed by burnt split ends. She was hoping to start a trend in the kingdom and did try issuing a proclamation declaring this decade the "Eh, so-you-didn't-have-time-to-wash-or-style-it-so-stick-it-up-in-a-ponytail" Decade, but her loyal subjects were most resistant to following this fashion statement.

And now it was time for the Royal Ball. Her firstborn princelie had been scoping the Kingdom chicks and was going to pick out his own lovely. What should the queen wear? She surveyed her shapeless, worn, princess-duds and could find nothing appropriate. As she tried on various items, that pesky full-length mirror kept saying, "Who's the fairest of them all? Certainly not YOU, my dear!" Her hair was a shambles, her face a lumpy mess, her teeth like aged wood—and not in a good way.

Then and there our fair maiden sent out an emergency proclamation. "From here on and henceforth, I shall get my act together and reclaim my fair beauty!" And all the Kingdom Personal Trainers and all the Kingdom Beauty Consultants were summoned. And after six months of great effort, the fair princess emerged at the Royal Ball. And her husband, who had been away in a far country, dropped his jaw and exclaimed, "Oooooh, baby! That's *my* princess! I'm picking her!" And all the kingdom clapped and were happy and the charming prince and the renovated fair princess lived happily, and attractively, ever after.

Now you may think that this is a funny fairy tale, but sadly for many of us, it is painfully close to the truth. It never ceases to amaze me that so many women let themselves go and yet expect their husbands to simply tolerate their deteriorating appearance. As a wife, we need to do our utmost to try to keep ourselves attractive and appealing to our husbands. They are human. They are normal. They are not attracted to slovenly appearances. They may love you dearly, but we owe our husbands our valiant efforts in taking care to keep ourselves healthy and attractive.

Let's conduct a little experiment. Close your eyes. Go ahead. Close them. Well, you better read this paragraph first and *then* close them. Now *in your mind* look in the mirror at yourself and see the *real* you—not how you look right now—look at how you believe your spirit looks. What do you look like? Look up and down carefully.

That is how you want to be.

But be realistic: you will never look like you did in your early twenties. That is not the question. It is how do you look right now, at this age? Don't be unrealistic and say you want to weigh what you did when you got married (unless you're a newlywed!). And don't just consider weight issues—what does your mental image look like in all aspects of appearance? That is your goal.

Elder Hanks said, "For any choice daughter of God the maximum effort to keep active, to build a strong base of good and vibrant health, to work hard at conditioning and developing a healthy and attractive body—all are especially important."[4] I like how he describes it—"a healthy and attractive body." That does not mean we have to be a 10 percent body fat hardbody with abs of steel. It means that we do our best to maintain an attractive body and to keep it fit and healthy.

Let's face it. We all know what to do to improve our body. It's a matter of *doing*. And most of that begins in our head. You and I both know that all the good intentions in the world, all the bad feelings, all the lists, are completely a waste of time. The moment you truly decide, and I mean *really decide and commit,* is the moment you begin to change. All the rest is just prep-work.

Let me remind you of Mom's Best Advice number 7: "He's surrounded by babes at work. He doesn't want to come home to a slug." Never forget that there are plenty of attractive women wherever he goes; make sure he comes home to one.

Elder Hanks details six steps to attaining this goal.[5] They are a good review:

1. Physical activity is essential to good health.

This is a tough one for me because I'm not really a physical person. I've always been more of an "egghead." Please do not think that the only path here is working out at a gym with a bunch of hardbodies around who don't give you a second glance. There are many paths to physical activity.

Find *your* way to add physical activity to your life. It doesn't matter what it is. Find what works for you. Do you love dancing? Stick on a CD and dance your heart out around the house. Do you enjoy walking? This is the easiest one. I combine walking with praying, and it's wonderful. Of course the entire neighborhood thinks I'm an odd woman who talks to herself, but what else is new. I walk through a hilly area about three days a week. Frankly, I do it as much for my mental regeneration as my physical. Just remember to get good quality shoes (they're worth the money) and wear your sunscreen!

Are you social? Find a class or environment that fits. I found a workout class in an all-woman club that perfectly fits. The teacher is sixty (and she can do twenty one-handed push-ups without breaking a sweat—aaaarrrgh!) and the women are in their forties and fifties. It has been wonderful. I've been with this class for over eight years and work out there three days a week. I like it because they do both aerobics and weight training. Weight training is crucial if you're over thirty-five. Also, I am very competitive, so I find that I do much better in a group environment. When I'm alone, I tend to cop out.

Do you like to swim? Go find a year-round pool. Do you like to jump rope, jump on a trampoline, window-shop (just do it while speed-walking around the mall!), ride a bike, whatever? It is crucial that you find your own path of physical fitness. Also, it is important to mix it up. If you do not find what works for you, it will not work! You will hate every minute of it, and before long you won't be doing it.

My sister who is in her fifties took up running and does marathons. I absolutely despise running. I found my heaven in kick-boxing. Man, does it work out the aggression! My friend

Izzy is a senior with arthritis; she faithfully attends a water aerobics class, which has significantly improved her mobility and lessened her aches and pains. Wendy has several little ones and works out with videos at home. Find your favorites. Pick a couple. Rotate them.

If you're doing one thing and you don't enjoy it, switch! (Important tip: if you're considering joining a club, ask for a one-month trial before you pay that big enrollment fee. That way you can see if you like it.) Too many of us keep trying the same thing, hate it, and bomb out.

Walking can be made easier by listening to scriptures as you walk (you'll be fit *and* a scriptorian! Double threat!). Listen to fun music. Buy cute workout clothes. Do whatever you need to do to make it a habit.

I have to admit, it took me a long time to make it a habit. I would go to my workout class and when I got into my car to go home, I would literally clap my hands and shout, "Way to go, Merrilee! You did it! I'm so proud of you!" Yes, I'm sure the passersby were wondering about the psychopath in the van. But I did it every single time. Now it is to the point where I have to force myself *not* to go if I have a conflict, because it's so ingrained.

Begin every day with *movement* as your goal. Then build from there. Each day keep repeating, "Today I will *move* my body." As you go throughout the day, you'll be far more aware of your body. You can stand in line at the grocery store and rise up and down on your toes (fabulous for your calves, though you may look funny). Walk farther, take stairs, swing your arms. Begin moving it!

And when you do your formal exercise, applaud yourself when you're done. Compliment yourself. You may think it's silly, but such applause is heavy-duty programming that will absolutely have an impact on your sticking with it. And don't worry if people stare. They're just impressed. Yeah, that's it.

2. Watch what we eat.

Of course we know we need to watch what we eat. If only it were that easy. I'm very content to watch it—on my plate, going into my mouth—I'm watching away.

Many, many of us have trouble eating too much and eating too much junk. Let me add just a few ideas.

Remember, proper diet and nutrition starts in your *brain* first. Attitude is the most important eating strategy. The rest is just follow-through. I spent a year of high stress and didn't do a whole lot to work on eating fabulous nutrition. Why? Because I knew that my brain was totally overloaded and that I didn't have the brainpower to commit to proper eating. The next year, things calmed down and I was much better able to devote the neurons necessary to monitoring my diet.

Also, it helps to study the Word of Wisdom—not just read it, but truly study it. Insights and understanding will come to you. (Such as, "How is 'eat meat sparingly' compatible with the latest diet craze?") The Lord will provide you with promptings to help you eat healthy.

Next, write down all the strategies you know about. Come on, you know a slew of them. Drink eight cups of water a day. Eat your dinner on a salad plate. Eat a nutritious snack at 10:00 A.M., 4:00 P.M., and 8:00 P.M. Eat breakfast every day. Set your fork down between every bite. You can go on and on. You know a lot. If you don't, just get on the internet and type in "diet tips"—and brace yourself.

After you've written down all the strategies, pick the five that you think you need to work on the most or that would have the most impact. Then just start with number 1. Keep doing it for at least three weeks until you have mastered it and it has become a habit. Then move to number 2. This is far more effective than "going on a diet" because with this approach you are changing your nutritional habits, and those changes can then stick for life. If you need to work on a strategy longer than three weeks, no problem. Make it your top priority until you've mastered it. Don't start another until you've mastered the most important one.

It's crucial to structure a supportive environment, including one that is emotionally supportive. This may necessitate eliminating or restructuring friendships and relationships that are just not helping. You have friends who delight in pigging out? Perhaps it's time to go to the movies or shopping instead. Your kids make rude comments? Time to have a very clear family meeting where rules are established.

You need to set up a supportive physical environment as well. Move the cookie jar out of visual range and buy cookies you hate. Ditch the candy bowl entirely. Put all junk food in a box out of the way or in a different cupboard that you don't frequently use. Is your treadmill in a really hard-to-get-to spot? Find a better one. Examine your surroundings and ask what you could change that would be helpful and supportive to you.

Finally, pick a motivational method that will help you. I have found that this helps a ton. I love motivational books. I highly recommend *Awaken the Giant Within* by Anthony Robbins or *The Power of Full Engagement* by Jim Behr and Tony Schwartz. I'm reading Dr. Phil's book *Ultimate Weight-Loss Solution* right now, and it's helpful. Other people really enjoy motivational CDs. Some really benefit from a plan. Weight Watchers can help you have one. They are relatively inexpensive and allow you to eat real food, focusing on modifying habits. For those of you who are really, really busy, you can even participate online. The accountability of weighing in with a stranger is very helpful.

Motivational methods can really help give you the push and drive you need to tide you over.

Bottom line, be vigilant. This is an ongoing, lifelong commitment. And it's important.

3. Sleep.

Talk about starving yourself! I see so many sleep-deprived women it's incredible! They're young moms, incredibly overcommitted women who burn the candle at both ends, women dealing with menopausal sleep disruptions, you name it, walking zombies all.

A friend of mine claims to be able to survive on the four to five hours of sleep she gets every night. Balderdash. Your body can only handle that for so long before damage begins to occur.

It's always interesting to me to listen to the safety instructions while flying in a plane. They show how to use the oxygen masks and then say a very important thing: "If you are traveling with a child, you should give yourself oxygen first and then assist your child." I refer to this as the Oxygen-to-the-Parent-First Principle, and you'll see it creep up again in this book.

Think about how vigilant you are (or will be) that your children get enough sleep. We put them down for naps religiously; we make sure they go to bed on time. If they appear to be tired and dragging, we send them to bed.

Remember, Oxygen to the Parent First! Put yourself to bed! This is probably number 1 in importance in terms of caring for a woman's body. You can't do anything else if you're exhausted. And I have seen women literally spend decades like the walking dead.

Begin by getting eight hours of sleep no matter what. All else must end or must wait. Go to bed. And remember, naps are not just for children! I only get about 6–7 hours of sleep at night because of seminary, and so I faithfully take a nap; that gives me an average of eight hours a day throughout the week. People say that I'm the busiest person they know and cannot figure out how or why I take naps. I learned the importance of adequate rest at a young age. I wake up at 5:00 A.M. and then go 100 miles per hour until about 1:00 or 1:30 P.M. And then I take a nap. I sleep for about an hour or two (well, okay, usually closer to two!). Then I go full tilt until about 10:00 or 10:30 P.M.

Now you may be a lousy napper—then you *must* get those solid eight hours at night. When those babies go down to sleep, you go too! I don't care that you have a list a mile long. You will be far more effective if you get adequate rest. You won't be as crabby. You'll be far more efficient. You'll be slimmer and much, much healthier.

4. Take a break.

Elder Hanks next suggested taking a break. I've talked about this previously, so I'll just add a few ideas here. Do you enjoy cerebral activities such as reading a book, listening to music, artwork, or others? Do you enjoy physical activities such as going for a walk or swimming? What relaxes you? Make sure you take the time to stop the whirlwind and do it.

I always think of Mona while thinking of this principle. Mona was the biggest workaholic I ever met. Mona never took a break. She was always busy, always cleaning her clean house, always working on her lists. It was crazy! And her kids have very few memories of their mom ever taking any time to play or do anything spontaneous or fun. After many years, you could see the toll this was taking on Mona's body and face. She was a walking billboard for Botox—deep frown lines marked her face very early.

I call this "Martha-ing." Remember the story in the Bible where Martha is the workaholic. Martha complains to Jesus that her sister, Mary, is just sitting there listening to the Savior. Now obviously Mary was taking a break and doing what relaxed her. Smart woman! But Martha was just teed off because she had not authorized a break-time and was probably a little jealous that she herself was not able to (or chose not to) take a break. So when I get a little too obsessed with my to-do lists and working (okay, that's like every day), I make myself stop and take a break. I say out loud, "Okay, Martha, time to chill out."

5. Keep clean.

"Meticulous care of ourselves and our living place and possessions is a hallmark of self-respect and wisdom," says Elder Hanks.[6] Part of this, very simply, is keeping our bodies clean.

We've probably all seen women who could pay more attention to this detail. Keeping our hair and bodies clean is crucial to being attractive and healthy. Nothing is a bigger turnoff than foul breath and greasy hair. Let's give our hubbies a break!

6. Cultivate a cheerful attitude.

I've seen many women who were—how shall I say this kindly?—not very endowed with physical beauty. (In fact, I would include myself in that category.) And yet I've seen those same women look absolutely radiant. How? A smile does more to make a woman beautiful than anything else she does. I've seen their faces glow.

Nowhere is this more true than in the temple. You see those temple workers who are often older women, and they're certainly not ravishing by worldly standards. But every time they break into a smile I can't help but think, "Well, aren't you just lovely!" My big goal in life is to have my face wrinkle in a smile.

And nothing can make a woman more unattractive than a sour attitude. I know toxic personalities like this, and I avoid them like the plague. Over time, that shows in every line of their face.

Practice being cheerful. Practice opening up your face and

keeping a pleasant expression. That will make you positively irresistible.

Along with a cheerful attitude is feeling love and appreciation for our bodies. I read an interesting book written by a Native American who spoke of the spiritual elements of his culture, and he told how every day he appreciated his body. He felt grateful for his arms and his legs and his hands and his feet and felt love for his body every day. What a wonderful attitude. So on days when I'm feeling somewhat lumpy, I begin a "thankful" prayer and thank Heavenly Father for all my parts that are working. I have several friends with disabilities, so I truly do feel blessed and feel love for my body.

Along with Elder Hanks's wonderful suggestions, I'd like to add a few of my own related to helping us nourish our bodies.

Head and Hands

My sister Kathe taught a valuable principle to her daughters, and I learned from her as well. What is always visible on your body? Your head and your hands. So we need to pay particular attention to these. She taught her daughters to keep their nails clean and well-manicured, and she bought them kits and taught them how to care for their hands. She taught them to always keep their hair in style and attractive. I had always been a nail-biter growing up. But her comments rang true, and ever since I have invested in acrylic nails. I consider it an important investment in my appearance.

So how do your hands look? Could they use some work? You can do a manicure yourself or get them done very inexpensively at the local beauty college. And let me tell you, if you have age spots and can afford it, you can visit your dermatologist and have them frozen off. Works great!

How does your hair look? Are you still wearing the same style you did ten or twenty years ago? Find women who have a similar hair type and ask them who styles their hair. Find a hairdresser you trust. And then trust her! Mine would say, "Merrilee, no perms!" I'd whine, "But I've always had a perm." She would rap me on the head with her comb—well, not literally—and say, "Perms are OUT." Best haircut I ever got was one day when I was disgusted and walked in and said, "Okay, do what you want." Man, it looked great, took ten years off my face, and was new and different.

Also, think how your makeup is going. I've seen some frightening apparitions—white eyeliner (say what?), bright blue lines hither and yon, brown lipliner, rather comedic application of eyebrow pencil—and I think, "Honey, come on!" Go ahead and experiment with those friends who are selling makeup because they'll give you a more honest opinion. Go into those fancy department stores (after you've left your VISA card in the freezer) and have them go at it and learn what's new, what's flattering to you, and what went out twenty years ago. The best makeup tip I ever got was when I went to have a glamour picture taken for my husband. The makeup artist had the perfect foundation makeup—it was inexpensive and the best I'd ever had. I've used it for the last fifteen years.

Remember, head and hands stick out. Make sure they're easy on the eyes.

Clothes

It's time for a very scientific experiment. Go stand in front of your wardrobe. Now hold up each item and ask these questions:

"Does this fit?" If the answer is "no," set it aside. *Be ruthless.* If it does not fit (and I mean without lying down and inhaling deeply), *set it aside.*

"Is it damaged?" Shall I tell you of my friend Annamaria, who came to church more times than I care to count with a safety pin where the bottom button of the dress should have been? If it has holes, runs, stains, missing buttons, and so forth, set it aside.

And then the infamous Dork Test: "Does it make me look like a dork?" Oh, I well remember the day when I realized that I had some dorky clothes. I was watching a television show called *What Not to Wear,* and they were showing a woman and, of course, making fun of her out-of-date, frumpy clothing. I realized to my horror that I had several wardrobe pieces that were the same. I ran to my closet, held them up, and said, "Does this make me look like a dork?" Oh, my word. They did! I had to admit that the huge, rather tent-like, denim dress was out and did nothing to make me look the least bit shapely. The sweater with all the cutesy-pie stuff all over it just made me look enormous and like I was out of touch with the reality of my age. Those relaxed-fit (i.e., saggy bum), pleated (i.e., big bubble making my stomach look huge), tight-at-the-ankles pants made me look like my backside and gut were gigantic and that I was terribly imbalanced. It was time to lay them to rest.

What was funny is that I said to my dearest one, "Honey, I had the funniest experience today. I've been going through my closet and applying the Dork Test."

And he replied, "Want me to help?"

Now this was a bit funny because he *never* complains about a single thing that I wear. I thought, "Man, I sure would like his input."

So I said, "Okay." (That was very brave, don't you think?) And he added a few more items to the set-aside pile—including the black shoes that made me look like a Pilgrim. "But those only cost $5!" I protested.

"Well, they would be good for a costume," he diplomatically replied. And he was right. When I really looked at them, they *were* Pilgrim shoes! Square toe, buckles, and all.

A big factor in applying this test is checking to see if the clothing is attractive to your body style and to our standards. Let's talk body style first. Erika is short and very skinny. Jeannette is a larger woman with short legs. Louisa is tall and big-boned. Each of them should be wearing very different clothing, no matter what the style.

Louisa should never wear those tight skirts. Erika wouldn't be caught dead in hip-emphasizing jeans. Jeannette should not wear broad horizontal stripes. Now no matter what the style, we should stick with what looks best.

I have a long neck and broad shoulders like a linebacker. One year I finally had to face the fact that I should never, ever wear a boat-neck top. (That's the kind that's straight and cut open with a slit in the top.) It made my shoulders look twenty feet wide and my neck and head like a giraffe. Definitely unflattering. Now this year boat-neck and wide-necked tops are absolutely the rage. I tried one on just to double-check. Nope, still have the whole giraffe-gorilla thing going on. So I just don't buy any. My friend Diane has a fabulous neck and collarbones and is small-framed on top. She looks absolutely dynamite in those tops. Now I'm very tall so I look fabulous in long column dresses and in tailored jackets. Diane would look horrible in those because she's short. Dress to flatter yourself, no matter what the style. Learn what looks good and stick with it and avoid the unflattering styles completely.

If you haven't a clue, find a snappy dresser who's about your size and shape and either copy her or consult with her. I was trying to spruce up my clothes (which had gotten rather frumpy and Molly Mormonesque). I had always admired Ellen in my ward, who was a sharp dresser. So when I went shopping, I'd think, "Now would Ellen buy this?" That saved me! Often, I would think, "Gee, that's cute!" I would hold it up in the mirror and say, "Would Ellen buy this?" I'd think, "No way, she wouldn't be caught dead in this!" Gradually, my wardrobe evolved into a classier, more flattering look.

I knew I had succeeded when a woman in my ward approached me and said that her children told her she needed to dress better. Her teenage son was in my Sunday School class and told her, "You should dress like Sister Boyack. She always looks good!" I was stunned. I told her about my little secret. She knew Ellen too. So now two of us are asking, "Would Ellen buy this?" Ellen recently passed away from breast cancer and we miss her. Her classy style, however, continues to teach us.

And please remember to be modest. My seminary girls taught me, "Modest is hottest!" I must admit, I've seen enough oozing flesh in the last few years to last me a lifetime!

I always say, "Whew, too much sharing!" Remember, if you have to adjust your garments to wear it, *don't buy it!* Tops are shorter than they used to be and pants start lower, so we must be vigilant. Just the other day a friend was commenting that she spent an entire ward activity staring at a woman's underwear because she was gesturing and her top didn't stay down far enough. So swing those arms all over the place and check. Sit down and check. Walk around and make sure you're modest.

Also, don't forget to get some cute date-night clothes. About once a year I force my husband to go shopping with me and help me pick out things that he finds attractive for me to wear on date-nights. It makes a huge difference.

Finally, with respect to clothes. Don't think it has to cost a lot. My sisters shop at thrift stores vigilantly, and they are *very* sharp dressers. There are very inexpensive stores out there. Use them. I do. You can look great and not break the bank in the process.

As we close our discussion of this section, remember one thing. You need to nourish your body for *you*, not just your husband. You want to feel good about yourself. You want to feel fit and healthy. It is worth every ounce of effort. And while you're in this process, you will teach your children the importance of health, fitness, and respecting yourself. Your body is a gift from God; do not neglect it.

Nourish Your Mind

Elder Hanks reminds us: "The mind, too, needs exercise."[7]

Oh, great, just when you thought we were finally past the E-word!

Yes, indeed, let us talk about nourishing your mind. In our family, we've given our sons a rule for dating and marriage: "No dumb chicks." I watched my oldest son date many that fell into this category and wondered how in the world he could do that after he'd been trained so carefully. Finally, he wrote me one day and said, "I've had it with dumb chicks! I'm going to look for someone with a brain." For him, that consisted of a good conversationalist and someone who was aware of what was happening in the world.

Now frankly, IQ is not the important factor here. Most people have bright minds. But give me a woman who is always learning and improving over a genius IQ any day of the week!

Some women feel that when they finish their education or get married they're done with learning. At that point, their brains begin to shrink. Excuses abound:

"I don't have time to read."

"I was never any good at school. I'm glad I'm out."

"I need to focus on my family now."

"What am I supposed to do? Sit down and read a textbook?"

"I don't have time." "I don't have time." "I don't have time."

I always find that excuse fascinating. "Oh, didn't you get that bonus three hours the rest of us got?" The real answer is, "I am not making this a priority. I am choosing *not* to learn."

Ask yourself, are you happy with your brain? Do you feel like you're learning and growing?

Again, it's a matter of respecting ourselves. We cannot starve ourselves mentally and expect to be attractive or capable. Elder G. Homer Durham wrote: "The responsibility to learn has greater significance for woman today than ever before. . . . Woman has not only to learn, but also to use wisely that which she learns; she must exemplify and teach well the ultimate and intimate things."[8]

Opportunities abound for developing our minds. President Spencer W. Kimball wrote: "It is a great blessing to be a woman in the Church today. The opposition against righteousness has never been greater, but the opportunities for fulfilling our highest potential have also never been greater.

"What is our greatest potential? Is it not to achieve godhood ourselves? What are the qualities we must develop to achieve such greatness?"[9]

He then listed several items to help us develop our mental potential.[10]

1. Gain intelligence, light, and knowledge.

President Kimball urged us to increase in our intelligence, light, and knowledge. Heavenly Father has encouraged us to gain intelligence and indeed stated that it is the only thing to go with us hereafter. The Lord said in Doctrine and Covenants 25:7–8, speaking to Emma Smith, "Thou shalt be ordained under his hand to expound scriptures, and to exhort the church, according as it shall be given thee by my Spirit. For he shall lay his hands upon thee, and thou shalt receive the Holy Ghost, and thy time shall be given to writing, and to learning much." The Lord then says that this is written to all women (see verse 16). We are encouraged to write and to learn much. Are we doing that?

I love Brigham Young. He had an incredibly enlightened view

of women, particularly for his day. President Brigham Young said regarding the education of his daughters, "I would not have them neglect to learn music and would encourage them to read history and the Scriptures, to take up a newspaper, geography, and other publications, and make themselves acquainted with the manners and customs of distant kingdoms and nations . . . ; in fine, let our . . . girls be thoroughly instructed in every useful branch of physical and mental education."[11] Great advice for women then and now.

But how do you nourish your mind? Again, find a plan that works for you. Here are some ideas that may help:

Begin with the obvious—reading. Start reading—almost anything! But spare your brain from junk. Ask yourself, do I really want this in my head forever? Read the classics, read magazines, read the newspaper, read the scriptures or Church books. Carry a book with you everywhere. Do you realize that if you read only four pages a day you'll read all the scriptures except the Old Testament in a year? Great recommended reading lists are available on the internet and at the high schools. Some books are pudding and some are chewy. Pick a chewy one every once in a while!

For those who don't like reading, or want to mix it up, there are incredible resources in tapes and CDs. Your local library is a wonderful source for these. The internet has a ton available. Every day I listen to a conference talk off the internet.

Take a class. Many free (or very inexpensive) classes are offered in your community. There are internet classes as well. BYU offers many classes on the internet for free or very little money (see ce.byu.edu). I think of Sister Kimball, who made this a lifelong habit and experienced great learning as a result. I think of my mom, who went back to college when I was in first grade and graduated with her degree at the age of fifty. My niece, Krystal, took flower-arranging and learned a wonderful skill. My sister Kathe took Parent Effectiveness Training and was able to turn it into a part-time career. I took six weeks of Spanish and loved it. I learned just enough to annoy my children. It's also very fun to take a class with your husband or with a friend. One year my husband and I took conversational Japanese for six weeks. I only remember how to say "hello," "please," and "thank you," but it was a blast taking it with him.

Think of a topic you love. World history? American literature? Quilting? Nutrition? Nuclear physics? *Study!* Take five minutes a day and cruise around on the internet, pick up a textbook, go to the library, wherever. I love to borrow my kids' textbooks and just read a chapter. It's wonderful and can lead to some fun discussions.

Think of a dash of light. So often we think, "Gee, I don't have any time to take a class or to read a big book." Well, that is your choice. So think about just a brief dash of light. You can sprinkle in learning in little bits and it adds up. Buy a bathroom book. Have you ever seen these? They have summaries of the classics in three or four pages. Carry something in your car for those little bits of time. Even that little effort accumulates over time, and you will have increased learning that will surprise you.

One day I was at the grocery store, and I saw a realtor and commented to the cashier that you could tell she was a realtor a mile away (just the whole dress and demeanor thing screamed "realtor"). He agreed. Now I was in a casual top and jeans and I said, "So what do you think I do?"

He replied, "I don't know but I figure you're a professional."

I was shocked because I certainly didn't look like one. "Why do you say that?" I asked.

He replied, "You use a big vocabulary."

Interesting. Education, in all its forms and in all its little bits and pieces makes a difference. Education is never a waste—and it's not just for kids!

2. Develop leadership.

Another purpose of our mental development, according to President Kimball, is to develop our leadership abilities. President Gordon B. Hinckley concurs: "The whole gamut of human endeavor is now open to women. There is not anything that you cannot do if you will set your mind to it. You can include in the dream of the woman you would like to be a picture of one qualified to serve society and make a significant contribution to the world of which she will be a part."[12] Our prophet has encouraged us to reach higher and to improve our mental abilities and our ability to serve and lead. In fact, President Hinckley told the members of the National Press Club, "People wonder what we do for our women. . . . We get out of their way."[13] It's true that the Church gives us extraordinary opportunities to develop our leadership potential.

Elder Marvin J. Ashton said: "Both home and family life and community service—either on a volunteer or paid basis—are within the grasp of the well-organized woman, each in its turn. A woman should feel free to go into . . . community service . . . when her home and family circumstances allow her to do so without impairment to them.

"This is a day when serious-minded, clear-thinking women are needed to promote a climate of peace, harmony, and righteousness in community life. . . .

"Let them make sure that they themselves are informed on the issues and their effect on the family and the community."[14]

How glorious a vision! Are we "serious-minded, clear-thinking women"? Are we learning and studying the issues in the community? Are we involved in our communities?

It is not enough to sit at home and just be good. We must be the salt of the earth. The power of a good woman in a position of leadership is immeasurable. I think of my friend Vicki, who has really grown in her leadership ability. And when she discovered that her child's middle school had a horribly inappropriate sex-ed pamphlet, she was able to rally hundreds and get the offending pamphlet removed. Libby would argue that she is not a leader, but I have seen her effective leadership as she served as program director of the local Cub Scout day camp and set a wonderful example of volunteerism and commitment. I, too, have had many, many experiences in serving as a leader in our community, and it never ceases to amaze me what one good woman can accomplish.

At one point I was called to be a stake missionary and did not have a clue. I really didn't know what a female stake missionary was supposed to do. I gave it much prayer and much, much pondering. One day while on my walk, an idea, a *huge* idea, was literally downloaded into my head. When I got home, I called the stake president and said, "President, I've been praying hard about what I'm supposed to do and I just had this idea. May I share it with you?" Well, eight short weeks later, we had organized our stake to present a nativity open house at our stake center to celebrate Christmas. In six of those weeks, volunteers from throughout the stake built a life-sized village of Bethlehem; and then we put together a display of over seven hundred nativity sets from around the world. We had musical presentations going on throughout the three-day event. We had a live nativity and actors in costume throughout the city of Bethlehem. All of this came from a simple idea.

One particular conversation still makes me chuckle. I phoned a man who had been assigned to help lead the security team, needing to discuss the details with him. He kept saying, "That's okay, Sister. Just tell me the brother who's in charge and we'll take care of it." I kind of didn't get that, so I kept discussing things. He interrupted me again. I went on. A third time he piped up, "Now, Sister Boyack, don't you worry. Just tell me who the brother is who's in charge and we'll take care of things."

I paused. "Well, I guess that 'brother' would be me!" He sputtered and was surprised. But bless his heart, he did a complete 180-degree turn and was completely supportive. I think he was just shocked that a woman was in charge.

One simple mom responded to inspiration and to the call to exercise leadership. What was the result? Over ten *thousand* visitors from all over San Diego County came to our stake center. Lives were changed. Whole families were converted. Some wayward souls came back.

Sisters, we cannot afford to be shrinking little violets anymore. We must extend ourselves and answer those calls to leadership. We must go out into our communities and lead. We have the Spirit. We have the intelligence, light, and truth. We must respond. Sheri Dew agrees: "We simply *must* understand this, because we *were born to lead.* By virtue of who we are, the covenants we have made, and the fact that we are here now in the . . . eleventh hour, we *were born to lead.* As mothers and fathers, because nowhere is righteous leadership more crucial than in the family. As priesthood and auxiliary leaders. As heads of communities, companies, and even nations. As men and women willing 'to stand as witnesses of God at *all times* and in *all things,* and in *all places'* (Mosiah 18:9) because that's what a true leader does. *We were born to lead.*"[15]

Our children are crucial in the Lord's plan. We must train them to be effective leaders as well. The best way is by example. Let us show them the way.

Realize that leadership takes many forms. It is not always the take-charge, rally-the-troops effort. Often, it is shown in quietly and firmly taking a stand for truth. Or in guiding our families. The Lord knows our gifts and abilities, and each of us will be called to lead in a way that uses them. We just need to be willing to respond to those promptings of the Spirit. Some of these opportunities may stretch us a bit, but the Lord knows us well and knows we are capable.

Now you may wonder what in the world this has to do with being a smart wife. As you rise to develop your brain and your intellect, as you rise to take those leadership opportunities, your entire marriage will be enriched.

3. Extend, exemplify, and teach in compassion and love.

President Kimball urges us to extend, exemplify, and teach in compassion and love as we develop our mental capacities. Sometimes we see women who have achieved success but who have turned harsh and masculine. Our gift and our strength is to bring our nurturing abilities to the world. We do not need to become men in order to grow mentally. We can use our own natural gifts of nurturing and love as we teach what we have learned. Rex D. Pinegar said, "Women have the seemingly innate ability to turn the harshness of our earthly existence into a world filled with softness, beauty and tenderness."[16]

As we teach and share what we have learned, we will continue to develop ourselves. This is a great benefit of being a mother. We can share and teach all the wisdom we have acquired over our lifetime and can continue to grow through that process as well.

Don't feel less worthwhile just because you're different from men. We are unique as women. We can use those strengths. As we also share our learning and our understanding with our husbands, we can do so in a way that exemplifies compassion and caring.

We can extend, exemplify, and teach with confidence.

Nourish Your Spirit

The Lord tells us to "lay aside the things of this world, and seek for the things of a better" (D&C 25:10). Never before was this more crucial counsel than it is in our day. We must seek for the things of a better world and nourish our spirits.

Sister Mary Ellen W. Smoot spoke of this: "Sisters, I wish I could place my hands on both sides of your faces, look deeply into your eyes, and impart to you a clear vision of your vital role as beloved daughters of God whose 'lives have meaning, purpose, and direction.' We are women who 'increase our testimonies of Jesus Christ through prayer and scripture study,' who 'seek spiritual strength by following the promptings of the Holy Ghost.' We 'dedicate ourselves to strengthening marriages, families, and homes' and 'find nobility in motherhood and joy in womanhood.' (Relief Society Declaration, in Mary Ellen W. Smoot, "Rejoice, Daughters of Zion," *Ensign,* Nov. 1999, 92–93) . . .

"When I hear sisters say, 'It is just too hard to do my visiting teaching' or 'I simply do not have time to pray and read my scriptures!' or 'I have too much going on to attend home, family, and personal enrichment meeting,' I want to say as President Hinckley has counseled, 'Rise to the great potential within you.' We may need to step back and consider if our actions are consistent with those things that matter most to us. As we place first things first in our lives, we can live each day without regret. . . .

"Yes, at times we are beset by troubles and pain and grief. But we must not surrender. We must not retreat. Eliza R. Snow, the second president of the Relief Society, penned these words:

" 'I will go forward. . . . I will smile at the rage of the tempest, and ride fearlessly and triumphantly across the boisterous ocean of circumstance. . . . And the *"testimony of Jesus"* will light up a lamp that will guide my vision through the portals of immortality, and communicate to my understanding the glories of the Celestial kingdom' ("The Lord Is My Trust," *Poems, Religious, Historical, and Political,* vol. 1 [1856], 148–49; emphasis in original).

"Oh, that I could look face-to-face into the eyes of every sister and have her catch the fire of those words and truly understand who she is and what she is capable of accomplishing. Oh, that the words of our declaration could take root deep within us: 'We are beloved . . . daughters of God. . . . We are united in our devotion to Jesus Christ. . . . We are women of faith, virtue, vision, and charity' (*Ensign*, Nov. 1999, 92)."[17]

Our testimonies as wives and mothers often carry our family to spiritual progression. It is as we share our testimonies that our children can grow their own.

In all the hullabaloo of our daily lives, we must pay particular attention to nourishing our spirits.

Think of your testimony about ten years ago. Now think of it today. Would you say it has grown?

Let's take a quiz to help assess how we're nourishing our spirits:

Quiz: My Spiritual Development

Scale of 1–10

- My relationship with the Savior is growing. I'm gaining in my understanding of the atonement. My love for Him is growing and deepening.

- I have regular prayer habits. Beyond that, I pray often throughout the day. My prayers are truly talking to my Heavenly Father and not just repetitious phrases. I feel that I'm communicating deeply with Him.

- I study my scriptures regularly. I go beyond reading them and truly ponder and pray about what I'm studying. I read the Book of Mormon every year.

- I ponder my temple and baptismal covenants and try to gain understanding of them and live them.

- I attend the temple frequently according to my circumstances. I've pushed myself beyond the easy amount of attendance to a level of attendance that requires me to stretch a bit.

Now it is very hard to measure spiritual things. Only *you* can know how you're developing and if you're feeding your spirit.

I'm intrigued by the story of Laman and Lemuel, who complained that they didn't get it when Lehi explained his vision. Nephi asks them why. Their answer: because they didn't go to the trouble to ask God!

We cannot grow spiritually without making an effort. Satan will make every effort to distract us. One of the biggest curses of an LDS woman is to be too *busy*—Being Under Satan's Yoke. Satan doesn't really need to get us to commit a big sin. He can be successful by getting us to just be too busy, and thus he accomplishes the same thing—spiritual deadening.

As we nourish our minds, we need to work on our internal spirituality, as contrasted with our external spirituality. There are Saints who can check off lots of boxes such as family home evening, check; read scriptures daily, check; always maintain a temple recommend, check—but they are critical and obsessive. Contrast them with the humble, repentant, faithful follower of the Savior who is filled with love for others.

The latter is considered a precious gift by her husband.

"Who can find a virtuous woman? for her price is far above rubies. The heart of her husband doth safely trust in her, so that he shall have no need of spoil. She will do him good and not evil all the days of her life" (Proverbs 31:10–12).

The path to nourishing the spirit is clear. The Lord says, "Keep my commandments continually, and a crown of righteousness thou shalt receive" (D&C 25:15). We are taught each week what to do. We know what we need to do. We just need to carefully and thoughtfully nourish our internal spirituality. As we do, we shall truly become a smart wife.

Nourishing your body, mind, and spirit. It's like watering a garden—you will be a source of beauty, good fruit, comfort, and joy. Not only will *your* life be improved and blessed, but your husband will be blessed, as will your family and everyone around you.

We cannot afford to starve ourselves any longer. Oxygen first to you, and then to your family.

Remember, the greatest way to gain the respect and love of your husband is to respect and love yourself. Allow the Real Me to shine and to grow. That's who he fell in love with—that's who he wants to be with forever.

NOTES

1. Marion D. Hanks, "Magic Aplenty," in *Woman* (Salt Lake City: Deseret Book, 1979), 102.

2. Hanks, "Magic Aplenty," 108.

3. Gordon B. Hinckley, "Standing Strong and Immovable," *Worldwide Leadership Training Meeting,* 10 January 2004, 21.

4. Hanks, "Magic Aplenty," 109.

5. For complete list, see Hanks, "Magic Aplenty," 109–11.

6. Hanks, "Magic Aplenty," 111.

7. Hanks, "Magic Aplenty," 111.

8. G. Homer Durham, "Woman's Responsibility to Learn," in *Woman* (Salt Lake City: Deseret Book, 1979), 33, 32.

9. Spencer W. Kimball, "Introduction," in *Woman* (Salt Lake City: Deseret Book, 1979), 2.

10. For complete list, see Kimball, "Introduction," 2–3.

11. Brigham Young, in *Journal of Discourses,* 26 vols. (Liverpool: Latter-day Saints' Book Depot, 1854–86), 9:189.

12. Gordon B. Hinckley, "How Can I Become the Woman of Whom I Dream?" *Ensign,* May 2001, 95.

13. Gordon B. Hinckley, *Discourses of President Gordon B. Hinckley,* 2 vols. (Salt Lake City: Deseret Book, 2005), 2:460.

14. Marvin J. Ashton, "Woman's Role in the Community," in *Woman* (Salt Lake City: Deseret Book, 1979), 92–93.

15. Sheri Dew, *No One Can Take Your Place* (Salt Lake City: Deseret Book, 2004), 64; emphasis in original.

16. Rex D. Pinegar, "Woman As a Teacher," in *Woman* (Salt Lake City: Deseret Book, 1979), 22.

17. Mary Ellen W. Smoot, "Steadfast and Immovable," *Ensign,* November 2001, 91, 92–93.

CHAPTER 5

But How Do I Change My Husband?

*The Lord in His wisdom knows that men and
women complement one another and has established eternal
marriage to help us reach our divine potential.*

P rincess, having had sufficient experience with princes,
seeks frog."

I would bet that each woman reading this has
reached a point in her marriage where she thought,
"Man, I have *got* to change my husband! Or this will never
work!"

You may think:

"He is so neat around the whole house, but his desk looks
like a hurricane hit!"

"He puts ketchup on chicken pot pie. Who in their right
mind does that?"

"I knew he liked sports, but this is ridiculous!"

"He likes country music—I mean a lot!" (When my
youngest was about nine, he came to me after school
with a long face. "Mom, I had to break up with my girlfriend today." "Uh, okay," I responded—having no idea
that he even *had* a girlfriend. "Why?" "Well, she liked
country music," he replied gravely. "It would have never

worked out." "Probably a wise choice," I replied. "There are some things that are just not negotiable.")

And then one thought that I bet most women in the Church have had: "I thought he was devoted to the gospel. He's a returned missionary, after all. But his idea of devotion and mine are vastly different. If I didn't do family home evening and family prayer, it wouldn't get done. Isn't he supposed to be the patriarch?"

Then there are some scary ones:

"He's addicted to pornography. I catch him at the computer all the time and it makes me sick."
"I think he's doing cocaine. I'm not sure, but I think so."
"The kids are terrified of him. When his temper blows, we're all terrified. How can we live like this?"
"I think there's another woman. I don't want to accuse him if it isn't true, but I'm worried. There are some scary diseases out there."

Any time we enter into a relationship, we have to deal with the attributes and behaviors of others that affect us. Some can be a pain and some can be very serious. And we spend a lot of our time wondering what we can do about it.

If you are experiencing abuse, *go to your bishop*. I don't care how embarrassed you are. Get a blessing immediately. Have enough backbone to protect yourself and your children. Today is a good day to give him a call.

Also, consider counseling. Your bishop can give you a referral. Often women say, "Well, he won't go to counseling." Okay. There's not a whole lot you can do about that. So *you* go. You need the help, and counseling will help you. Take care of yourself and go.

But most of us just have the day-to-day difficulties. Little irritants. How to we handle those?

Bottom line, *How can I change my husband?*

Let's First Get Rid of the Stupid Stuff

You know what your stupid stuff is—those little irritants that wear on you like sand in your shoe. Go ahead—make a little list if it will make you happy. But how do we get rid of it?

First, let's talk a little perspective here. Many women gripe if their husbands leave the toilet seat up. Now can you imagine my husband and four sons saying, "Why does she always leave that toilet seat down? Doesn't she care about me? I have to lift it up like every time! Don't you think that's rather selfish of her?" Do you think those words would ever cross their lips? Not a chance. That's because most guys realize that small stuff is . . . dare I say it? *Small.* They flip up the seat, do their business, and do not give one thought to mentally berating their wives for their apparent insensitivity.

If you have these kinds of concerns, realize that they are silly, small, stupid—and choose to *let them slide.*

There was once a story in the *Ensign* that talked about this situation, which the author called "The Grapefruit Syndrome." The woman, who had been married for only two years, said she had been reading a magazine (always a dangerous source of marital advice). She told her husband that the magazine recommended that married couples talk about the complaints they had about one another in order to help them resolve their differences. Her husband reluctantly agreed to go along. She went first. She relates, "After more than fifty years, I remember only my first complaint: grapefruit. I told him that I didn't like the way he ate grapefruit. He peeled it and ate it like an orange! Nobody else I knew ate grapefruit like that. Could a girl be expected to spend a lifetime, and even eternity, watching her husband eat grapefruit like an orange? Although I have forgotten them, I'm sure the rest of my complaints were similar.

"After I finished, it was his turn to tell the things he disliked about me. Though it has been more than half a century, I still carry a mental image of my husband's handsome young face as he gathered his brows together in a thoughtful, puzzled frown and then looked at me with his large blue-gray eyes and said, 'Well, to tell the truth, I can't think of anything I don't like about you, Honey.'"[1]

Rather than nitpick our husbands to death and be overly concerned over such minor things, let's choose instead to just set them aside and not fret about them anymore. And when they come up in your head, mentally shut that thought down and say, "Nope. I'm not going to even worry about this because it's so small and inconsequential." And then immediately think of something else.

But let's talk for a moment about shared things. These are the things that both of you use, like perhaps a tube of toothpaste. I have an incredible life-altering tip on how to handle these things: *Buy your own!* Get your own toothpaste, your own Kleenex box, your own place to put your keys, whatever. Splurge. It'll solve a lot of fretting time.

A couple of years ago I attended a wedding. In counseling the young couple, the man performing the wedding told them it was time to put away single things and to now have joint things. He said it was time to get rid of their separate bank account and get a joint bank account. At this point, I wanted to leap up and scream, "Whattaya nuts? That practically killed my marriage!" However, I don't think people are used to people jumping up and screaming, "Whattaya nuts?" during a wedding ceremony, and so I very carefully restrained myself. Later, my mom-in-law said she was watching me to see if I would do it! She complimented me on my great self-control.

In deference to this good marriage officiator, many things in marriage are wonderful if jointly done. However, you can have separate things and still have a good marriage. At the top of my list for many couples is having separate bank accounts and separate credit cards. For many of us, this is the key to financial sanity. We have ours set up so that I handle most of the household bills out of the family account (where the bulk of my husband's paycheck is deposited); then he has a separate account where part of his paycheck is deposited, and he handles certain other bills, including our date night. We have separate credit cards, and never the twain shall meet. This was crucial, because I'm a spender married to a spender. Spenders should definitely *not* share bank accounts! Otherwise they have a giant slush fund to draw from without the accountability and responsibility to control themselves. For other couples, having joint accounts works just fine. For some couples, having the same bathroom works great, but for others, separate bathrooms may solve a lot of problems. Each situation is unique, but remember that you do not have to hold everything jointly to have a great marriage.

So let go of the small stuff; and if you're sharing and it's bugging you, buy your own.

Now, we just took care of 5 percent of his faults. We're making progress!

Understanding Complementary Gifts

Several years ago, I was sitting in a class at Education Week with the Ya-Ya's. (We were having our girls' week and loving it!) Bernell Christensen was teaching and made a statement that intrigued me: "Every family has all the spiritual gifts it needs to reach exaltation."[2] I don't remember much else of what he said because that comment caught my attention. (Sorry, Bernell, if my mind wandered after that!) I thought about it, repeatedly turning it over in my mind. I don't think it was a radically new concept, but for some reason I began to chew on it. I pondered that thought for months.

That fall, our family was driving home from the hills of Julian, where we had attended church at the local LDS branch. Out of the clear blue, a question came to my head: "Do you trust your husband spiritually?"

I recognized that the Spirit was calling. I thought, "What? Huh?" (which is my usual keen response to promptings from the Spirit).

The question was repeated: "Do you trust your husband spiritually?"

Well, that's certainly an odd question, I thought. So I began to mull it over. Did I? I thought of a friend of mine who is quite a scriptorian. She had determined that this equaled righteousness. Since her hubby did not meet *her definition* of righteousness, she felt that he was not righteous enough. She even went so far as to say that she would be assigned to another man in the hereafter. What balderdash!

But I realized that I had been doing the same thing. For twenty years I had not trusted my husband spiritually. To me, spirituality equaled strict obedience. This is the very thing that I'm good at—I try to obey quickly and without question, while Steve sometimes comes along more slowly. I had criticized my scriptorian friend for picking out one thing she was good at and using it to define righteousness—and now I suddenly realized I had been doing the same thing. I had created my own definition of righteousness and then had measured my husband against it. And I thought he came up short. I was rather humbled to see my error in perception clearly for the first time.

Then the Spirit asked me, "What gifts does your husband

have?" I thought for a few minutes. Then I got out a pad of paper and began to write. He has integrity, honesty, love for his family (about the best husband and father I've ever seen), and loyalty. He's true, has patience, temperance (thank goodness, because I do not!), kindness, and humility. He has the gift of a testimony of Christ. He had many other gifts, and I kept writing. (Now of course at this point I'm a weeping mess and poor Stevie is making furtive glances at me and my growing list. Like any normal husband, I'm sure he was thinking, "Oh, great, I'm gonna get it now. She's obviously writing down stuff she wants me to correct . . . " Poor dear.)

Clearly, his gifts are *different* from mine. In areas where I'm weak, he's strong. In areas where I am strong, he is weaker. I have terrible difficulty in not being critical of others. He rarely has a problem with that. I'm somewhat of a scriptorian; he is less so. He is humble; I am less so. (Okay, I'm being soft on myself. I'm a *lot* less so!) It was amazing as I compared our gifts to see the correlation. For some reason, I hadn't seen that before.

So do I trust him? I had learned that every family is given all the gifts they need as a *unit* to gain exaltation. So do I trust him to use his gifts to get us back to our Heavenly Father? Yes, because a banana will always be a banana. Steve will always be Steve—with all *his* gifts. It's who he is. He will always be loving, humble, patient, and easy-going because that's who he is. He will use his gifts to bless our family and our marriage. I will use my gifts as well, because that's who I am and that's what comes naturally to me.

So do I trust him spiritually? For the first time in twenty years, the answer was a resounding *yes!* I have really struggled with pride and judgment. He hardly ever has a problem with either. He's struggled with other things that I've hardly ever had a problem with. Together we have the gifts we need to return *together.*

I have been critical because he didn't have *my* gifts. Rather, I should have been grateful. I cannot gain exaltation alone. *I need his gifts and he needs mine.*

So the next question was—do I trust *us,* our marriage, to make it spiritually? Yes. For the first time in over twenty years, I believed that *we* could make it back *together.*

For the first time in my life—*I had a testimony of my marriage.*

It was the first time in twenty years that I *understood and completely valued* my husband. I had spent twenty years wanting, demanding, expecting him to be just like me. I finally understood that I *needed* him to be just like he is. It was a miraculous understanding that transformed the way I looked at my husband and my marriage.

The Lord wants us to *become one.* And so He says, "Now Merrilee, you help Steve with this; and Steve, you help Merrilee with that." Together we are *whole;* together we are *one.* Part of this is male-ness combined with female-ness to a level we probably don't fully comprehend. The Lord in His wisdom knows that men and women complement one another and has established eternal marriage to help us reach our divine potential.

You may go through this process yourself. Get out your patriarchal blessings and list each of your spiritual gifts. List gifts you have learned about directly through the Spirit. Compare each of your roles. Read the proclamation on the family to understand your roles better. You will see that you fit together like two puzzle pieces. And then, hopefully, you will come to the same point I did.

You will stop demanding that he *be like you.* And that is a major breakthrough. Elder Neal A. Maxwell spoke of this in, of course, his perfect alliteration: "Brethren, marry someone who is your better in some respects; and, sisters, do likewise, so that your eternal partnership is one of compensating competencies."[3]

Complementary gifts or compensating competencies. It all means that some of your husband's differences may be a good thing. Elder Russell M. Nelson states, "An ideal marriage is a true partnership between two imperfect people, each striving to complement the other, to keep the commandments, and to do the will of the Lord."[4]

It's interesting to see what happens when you truly understand this principle. Perhaps your husband is very outgoing and you are more reticent. So when you're at a party and he's yapping with everybody in the room, rather than be disgusted and wonder why he always does that, you'll stop and think, "Oh, thank goodness! It's a good thing he's outgoing because I'm not. If we were both as reticent as me we'd end up spending all our time at home with no friends!" You'll look at things so differently. You'll appreciate the fact that he's organized and detail-oriented when you're comfortable in chaos. You'll look differently at the fact that he is solid and steady when you're emotional and panicking.

Once your eyes have been opened, you'll begin to observe this in the marriages around you. You'll realize that your mom was the strict one and your dad was the softie and that the balance was very effective. You'll chuckle when your sister is the shopaholic and her husband a bit of a Scrooge. You'll see the complementary gifts in action, even if they don't realize it. In my marriage, I'm the hyper one and my husband is the steady one. In my girlfriend's marriage, she is the steady one and her husband is hyper. We have often commented that if I married Tom, we would have blown up in a year and if Steve had married Diane, they would have gotten nothing done! It isn't necessarily that opposites attract, it's that the puzzle pieces fit.

Then there is the further blending of gifts with your children. You begin to see that the various strengths and abilities complement one another so that the entire family has a good mix. We need to be grateful for that blending both in our marriages and in our families and allow all those gifts to work together rather than insisting on clones. As we change that focus, family members are free to develop their own gifts and to discover new ones along their path. We also learn to rely on each other more, both in our marriage and our family, and to appreciate the differences rather than struggle so much against them.

This brings us then to the Seesaw Principle. Married couples live on a seesaw. They are happiest when the seesaw is at equilibrium—that point where both sides are balanced. If one is way up and the other down, they will seek to even things out so the seesaw once again becomes level and balanced.

Complementary gifts are one way that couples achieve equilibrium. Where one spouse is weak, the other is strong so that the marriage remains in equilibrium.

But the Seesaw Principle is broader than that. It also covers the balance of emotion and intensity as well. To illustrate this principle, let me share a few examples I have observed.

Andrew has two children by a previous marriage. His children both began to go wayward and wandered down sinful and dangerous paths. As this played out, Andrew became more and more upset, which of course is normal. He felt guilty. He felt deep anguish. He felt a great deal of emotional upset. As he progressed, I watched his wife, Anna, become more and more quiet and solid and just as steady as a rock. I knew that she had no idea what she was doing. She was operating under the Seesaw Principle. As Andrew was flying high on emotion, Anna was going low and solid to the ground in order to balance him out. Over time, he began to cope better and she became her more animated, usual self.

Another couple illustrated this as well. Marta had serious health issues and struggled to cope with them. Her husband Jose was very supportive and helpful. As Marta grew more unable to cope with the demands of the household, Jose went into over-drive cleaning and organizing. He really stepped up to the plate in helping Marta, taking over many of the family responsibilities she was unable to deal with. This allowed the family to be balanced during this time of stress. He also began to try to improve his own health by running and biking. Eventually, he entered a triathlon. Balance achieved.

Couples will consciously or unconsciously try to achieve equilibrium. Look at the marriages around you and observe, and it will astound you.

Not only does this understanding help you in your marriage, but it is incredibly powerful to know as a wife. Why? You can help temper the up and down swings of the seesaw all by yourself. Remember when you were a girl and you were on the seesaw and the other person would sit way back so that you couldn't go up? You'd get so frustrated! You have the power to sit way back in your marriage so that your husband won't fly out of control. (Husbands can do the same thing in reverse.)

This is a powerful tool. Let's say something happens with one of your children. How you react will govern whether you go up or down on the seesaw, and it may also influence how your husband will react as well. Let's say you usually would absolutely freak out. Understanding the Seesaw Principle, you realize, "If I freak out, my husband will go into hyperdrive, taking charge and trying to solve everything." If you do not want that reaction, you can choose to modify your own. If you tone yourself down, he too will likely have a much more level reaction.

Be careful with this understanding, because it is so powerful that you might be able to use it to manipulate your husband. As I said, caution is important.

I used this tool a lot while my husband was out of work. I knew that he needed to be able to vent some of the frustration and fear he felt. As a result, I often kept a lid on my reactions.

I also knew that he needed to flip out a bit now and again. If I gave him a really mellow, "Yeah, whatever" reaction, he would go more into emotional intensity. When I felt that it was enough, I would ratchet up my own emotion. He would then back down in order to help and support me.

Understanding this allowed me to be more aware of my emotions and his reactions and helped me stay calm throughout a lengthy time of looking for work. If I had not understood this, I would have been freaked out for the whole time. Then, my poor husband, in order to help support me and to balance out my intense emotions, would have had to be calm, cool, and collected the whole time. Add that to the burden of emotion that he was feeling anyway, and he might have gone belly-up.

Do you see how this works? So you are upset that your husband gets all strong and controlling? Then cut back on being emotional and weak. He may simply be balancing you out! In most cases, if you come on a little stronger and in control, he will back down to keep equilibrium. If he is always weak and doesn't take charge, he may be balancing you out. If you didn't understand this, you might ramp it up and get more and more demanding and bossy and controlling. Instead, now that you know, you say, "Ah! I understand. I'll just back off." As soon as you do, the balance will shift and he'll exert himself more.

But I know it's hard to control yourself. You're thinking, "It'll never work! It'll never work!" Just hold back longer. Over time, he will increase his strength. You just have to resist the urge to jump in and ramp up your emotional reactions.

As I said, be careful with this understanding, and prayerful. You have much control, and you cannot use it unwisely. But your eyes will now be opened to the pull of that state of equilibrium.

Your kids go through the same thing. Ever notice how when one is gone, the others kind of switch positions and jockey things around a bit? Why? There is also equilibrium in the family, and they'll shift to accomplish just that.

So be patient. Use this tool wisely and well, and it will be a blessing to your marriage. As you gain more and more under-standing, your marriage will stay more and more in a state of equilibrium. This doesn't by any means mean boredom. But it does mean a whole lot less conflict, and that's a good thing.

So remember his gifts are there to complement yours, and vice versa. And remember that your marriage will achieve equi-librium one way or another. A smart wife uses this understanding to appreciate her husband and keep balance in the marriage. She makes balance work *for* them rather than against them.

Aha! We just resolved another 60 percent of those things you want to change. We're up to 65 percent!

Study the Attributes of Husbands and Men to Understand Them Better

To improve your marriage you need to understand what makes your husband tick. Men are very different from women, as I'm sure you've noticed by now. If you were going to enter into a relationship with a company, you would study it thor-oughly first. Now that you're in a marriage, it is really helpful to study and learn about men. There is a wealth of information on how men think and how they act and react. So learn a bit. Read and study.

Yes, this is rather unusual advice. I'm suggesting that you do "guy" homework!

As you study and learn about what a man is and how his head works, you will also learn what works and what doesn't work.

I was watching Dr. Phil on *Oprah* one day. (I, of course like all of you, *never* watch any daytime television. Only PBS. But I was probably recuperating from major surgery or something and happened to turn on the TV—yeah, that's it.) He was interviewing a married couple. The woman, who had previously been obese, had lost a lot of weight. Her husband was still heavy. And the woman was ticked off about it. So she had been ragging and nagging and nothing was working. Dr. Phil turned to the woman and said, "Is that working for you?" I *love* that question.

She stopped dead in her tracks. "Well, not really, but . . . " and repeated her tirade.

Dear Dr. Phil repeated his question, "Is that working for you?" She had to admit that it was not.

And then he turned to the husband and asked how he felt about her tactics and her request that he lose weight. The husband was in an incredibly defensive physical posture and basically said that there was no way he was going to lose the weight and he'd do whatever he wanted and she had better lay off because he was *not* going to let her force him to do a thing.

I just sat there amazed. This woman did not have a clue about how men work! She was in La-La Land if she thought ragging and nagging were going to work. A simple understanding of guys would have helped her tremendously. But she didn't even realize what she didn't know.

Well, it's our turn. Do we understand men? Do we know how their brains work? My friend Diane got married and wanted long, deep conversations with her sweet husband. He would patiently listen as she rattled on and on her deepest feelings and emotions. Unfortunately, he didn't really have anything to say back. For a few years she kept poking and prodding. (Oh, how many of us have done this! I sure did!) Finally, one day Tom said to her, "Honey, I know you want deep analytical conversations, but I'm not that way. What you see is what you get. I really don't even *think* those deep analytical thoughts. I'm just pretty simple, and everything's on the surface." Well, bless her little heart if she didn't really, truly hear her husband. The light bulb went off in her head. She finally realized that he wasn't holding out on her. He was giving her his all. It was just different. And she finally got it.

Most men have what is called "segmented thinking." They are very linear in their thinking. They think about work when they're at work. They think about sports when they're watching or playing sports. They think about you when they're kissing you. Women, on the other hand, are continuous thinkers, and somewhat complex. So you, when you're kissing your husband, are thinking, "Now, did I turn off the oven already? Oh yeah, I need to wash Johnny's PE uniform and I need to check to see if Laura needs a ride . . . " and on and on your brain goes. Sounds familiar, doesn't it? We just assume that guys think the same way and they don't.

So when he's at work, he's thinking "work" and it's very difficult for him to think, "Gee, I should call my sweetie and see how she's doing." That would require a jump to the "wife segment." They can do it, but it's not terribly natural. So we interpret this and think that they don't care, they don't love us, and so forth. We take their brain functions and reactions personally. In fact, we're just ignorant. Studying and learning can help.

President Faust counseled his young granddaughters to understand the differences, "I have said that you are wonderful, special, and unique as women. Let me tell you why.

"Women seem to arrive at decisions in different ways than men do. I have noticed that your grandmother 'thinks' with her heart. My approach seems more logical. Your grandmother is concerned about how her decisions affect the people around her. Beverly Campbell talks about it this way: For a woman, 'her primary concern is what will be the greatest good for the greatest number of those around her. In value terms this would be called "care and mercy." For men the research indicated that the moral thought process was probably much more direct. It ⸦ boiled down to firm rules of right and wrong, black and wh. ("Understanding the Uniqueness of Woman," transcript of a talk delivered at Brigham Young University—Hawaii, May 1981, 2).

"Sister Campbell says: 'Could it be that we, each of us, man and woman, were endowed at the time of creation with two distinct but equally important traits, traits which are both essential and complementary and bound to be used together in wisdom for the greatest good of all mankind?' (Ibid., p. 5.)."[5] Understanding that men think differently from women and that this is good and helpful in marriage will help tremendously.

One of the basic understandings that is crucial in dealing with your husband is that we usually get the relationships we've created. Let me repeat that: *We usually get the relationships we've created.* What does that mean?

When you use negative power on your husband (i.e., force, nagging, whining, manipulation, and so forth), he will typically react with *fight, flight,* or *submission.*

So when you confront him with power he could react with *fight.* This is the husband who is aggressive and argumentative. He will fight back to defend himself or his position. These husbands can become abusive over time if a woman continues to attempt to use power or force. Now, granted, some husbands are abusive because of their own behavioral choices. They react with *fight* to many things. I do not want to suggest that you as the wife are causing him to choose to be this way. What I am suggesting is that if you are using force and power on your husband and triggering fights and arguments—and your husband is not normally this kind of a person—then you can examine what you're doing to cause or contribute to this reaction.

Another type of husband will react with *flight.* This is the husband who is gone a lot. He will attempt to escape as much as possible from the situation where you are using power. An example might be the husband who is a workaholic or the guy who golfs all the time or hangs out with his buddies. He will go to great lengths to avoid being home with you.

The other type of husband is the one who will react with *submission*. Some may view this man as a spineless wimp. He will duck his head, slump his shoulders, and say, "Yes, dear, anything you say, dear." He will give in to your use of power to avoid continuing conflict.

It has been interesting to watch the evolution of men in general. Decades ago, most husbands would fight back if their wife tried to use force with them. Then there were a few decades where most husbands would use flight; we have a whole generation of absent dads. This generation, we are seeing more of the *submission* types. These are young men who, by and large, have been raised with fairly strong mothers. (That's my generation. We grew up during the women's movement and as a result were raised with the notion that no man was going to tell us what to do! We've gone a bit overboard by telling them what to do instead!) So the young men learned early on that it was easier to give in to Mom and transferred that to their strong wives.

Recently, a bishop approached me after hiding out in the back of the chapel and listening to my presentation on "How to Change Your Husband." He said, "You have no idea how true that is. We're having such a problem with weak young men. It's become a leadership problem. We're having a hard time getting these young men to show some backbone." Fascinating.

Elder Hugh W. Pinnock stated: "The first idea I suggest is fundamental: We must bring the Savior and his teachings into our homes and hearts. To really succeed, an eternal marriage must be Christ-centered. Though directed to priesthood bearers, the principles in Doctrine and Covenants 121 apply to both husbands and wives."[6]

And then he quoted verses 41, 42, and 45, which say:

"No power or influence can or ought to be maintained by virtue of the priesthood, [instead, power and influence can be maintained] only by persuasion, by long-suffering, by gentleness and meekness, and by love unfeigned; by kindness, and pure knowledge, which shall greatly enlarge the soul without hypocrisy, and without guile. . . .

"Let thy bowels also be full of charity . . . to the household of faith, and let virtue garnish thy thoughts unceasingly; then shall thy confidence wax strong in the presence of God; and the doctrine of the priesthood shall distil upon thy soul as the dews from heaven" (D&C 121:41–42, 45). These verses teach us much and describe so well the type of influence we should use rather than exerting force or power.

So how does your husband react to you? Remember, many women get only what they've created. So we need to be smart and when we see these reactions (*fight, flight,* or *submission*), back off. Remember the definition of stupidity—to keep doing the same thing over and over and expect a different end result. Like the ignorant woman who kept nagging and nagging her husband to lose weight and getting the same defiant reaction every time, we too need to examine our tactics.

President Hinckley, in comparing men and women, said: "Each of us is different. There must be respect for those differences, and although it is important and necessary that both the husband and the wife work to ameliorate those differences, there must be some recognition that they exist and that they are not necessarily undesirable. In fact, the differences may make the companionship more interesting."[7]

A good book that talks about these differences in men and women and will help in understanding is *Dealing with Differences in Marriage* by Brent A. Barlow.[8]

A smart wife seeks to understand how men think and then changes her behavior to accommodate those differences. Part of

109

this is just the awareness that those differences exist—and the decision not to take them personally.

Whew! That took care of another 5 percent! We're up to 70 percent!

Problem Ownership—Stop Owning His Problems and Let Him Grow

Another very powerful tool in being a good wife is understanding problem ownership. Women particularly have a problem with this. We think we have to own every problem that arises in the family. Somehow, we've gotten the notion in our head that if everyone's lives are not going perfectly, it's our responsibility to fix it.

So a huge understanding that is needed is that your husband has problems that are solely his own. He alone is responsible for fixing them—indeed, he *must* be responsible. Remember, many women get only what they've created.

Therefore, a wife needs to look at every issue and ask, "Who bears the responsibility for solving this?" If the answer is "my husband," *let it alone.* Oh, I know that this is extraordinarily difficult. But honestly answer that question. Don't say, "Well, gee, it affects me too!" Of course it does. Virtually everything your husband does or does not do affects you. That is not the criterion.

So I'll repeat. Who bears the responsibility for solving this? Whose problem is it?

He hasn't done his home teaching yet this month. Who bears the responsibility? He does. The garbage is piling up and it's his job. Whose problem? His. Things aren't going well at his job. Whose responsibility? His.

Instantly you must say to yourself (out loud if you're like me), "This is *not* my problem. It's his." Then you need to allow him the time and the space to fix it on his own.

Contrast this with the wife who bakes her husband goodies to take to his home teaching families so that he's manipulated into doing his home teaching so the food doesn't spoil. You know she's doing it to force him to go. Or the wife who in disgust drags the garbage out to the curb and then is furious with her husband all day. Or think of the wife who calls her husband's boss to complain about the way her husband is being treated at work. (An acquaintance of mine just did that. You can imagine the boomerang effect that had at home and at work.)

We must allow our husbands the great privilege and honor of solving their own problems. We may not force, nag, remind, cajole, ridicule, or manipulate. All of these are beneath us and certainly not the behavior of a smart wife. They do little to help solve the problem and may actually be counterproductive.

News flash. Your husband is not perfect. Yet. Give him an eternity to get there. (You're going to need the same.)

Ask yourself, how would you feel if he went after all your faults? Mad as a hornet! You know what your problems and faults are, and you'll fix them when you're darn good and ready. But aren't your faults affecting him? Certainly they are. However, most husbands usually don't complain nearly as much as wives do. Somehow, we feel "authorized" to fix him.

Face it, how did you feel reading the title to this chapter? You were likely licking your lips and clapping your hands in anticipation. You were going to fix all his problems, weren't you? Aha, guilty as charged!

Instead, learn this great skill. When problems creep up, say to yourself, "This is his problem, not mine. I am going to have faith in him and allow him the time and space to fix it."

If you have the courage and the intestinal fortitude to take this approach, an amazing thing will happen. When he realizes that you aren't going to nag, force, manipulate, or try to fix it, he is left to himself. He's probably not used to that. Rather than be defensive (which is usually what he resorts to for self-preservation), he can instead examine his problem himself and decide his course of action. He can decide if he wants to fix it or not.

Most of the time, he will fix it. It may take some time but he's bothered by his problems just as much as you are—probably more so. Let's face it, he *knows!* He was just resisting because you wanted it so badly. Or he was resisting because most of the time, you'd jump right in and solve it. So back out of it. Now!

Laurinda learned well. She announced to her husband, "Honey, I know that every month I nag you to do your home teaching, and I've realized that that was wrong. I'll never do it again. It's your responsibility, and I have faith and confidence in you that you'll do what's right."

Her husband was stunned. "Uh, couldn't you just remind me every month?" he pleaded.

"When was the last time you reminded me to do my visiting teaching?" she asked. End of discussion.

Guess what. He does it all the time now. Yes, occasionally it's in the last week, but she bites her tongue. Smart woman.

I called Debbie one day and she said she had been out mowing the lawn. I was shocked, "You're nine months pregnant! What are you doing mowing the lawn?"

"Well," she said, "if I didn't do it, it just wouldn't get done. It's the same thing with the garbage. He's supposed to take it out. I pile it all up by the door, and he'll just step over it and go off to work."

Well, let's just say that Debbie and I had a serious talk. She told me that she and her husband had agreed on household duties, but he wasn't doing his part. "Let me tell you," I chided, "that lawn and garbage could pile up nine feet high and I'd never touch it! Promise me you'll never touch it again." She reluctantly agreed.

Well, lo and behold, guess who is mowing the lawn and taking out the garbage? And yes, it piled pretty high and grew very tall before he realized that she was not going to break down and do it for him. Happy woman. Productive husband.

Some husbands will hold out for a long time, testing your resolve. Don't give in. Some husbands will try to get you to do things. Stand back. Repeat, "I have faith in you, honey!" Smile brightly. What a gift you will give him!

And sometimes, you'll find that when you let go of owning all his problems and focus on your own, his suddenly seem much smaller. They lose their emotional grip on you. Some will just fade away, and you'll think, "Man, why was I so bent out of shape over this?"

The shorthand version for experts at problem ownership is "NMP." That stands for Not My Problem. As things creep up, you just repeat over and over to yourself, "NMP . . . NMP." For many women, this is a life-changing skill.

Now I am not suggesting that we toss our spouses to the wolves and abandon all caring help. I would hope that when we back off and let them own their problems, we switch to a more supportive role. We can let them take ownership of their own problems and then be emotionally caring and supportive of them. This is very, very different from being the one in charge, demanding change. It is the role of a loving spouse who is there to help when needed but not to take over.

President Hinckley said, "I issue a plea for husbands and wives to respect one another and live worthy of the respect of one another, and to cultivate the kind of respect that expresses itself in kindness, *forbearance, patience, forgiveness,* and true affection, without officiousness or *show of authority.*"[9] Notice those words: "forbearance," "patience," "forgiveness," no "show of authority." All of them fit with this principle of problem ownership. Forbearance is a fancy word for bite your tongue! Have the patience as he works through his problems. Forgive him when he messes up or takes longer than you'd like. And hold back that show of authority which creeps up as forcing, nagging, whining, and manipulating.

As you let go of your husband's problems, he will truly begin to grow and develop. He'll face his own issues and learn to handle them himself. He'll ask for your advice and input as needed. Then you'll be true equal partners. And he'll think you're the perfect wife. Of course, we knew that you were.

But wait, that's the last 25 percent—oh, fine! You're telling me there's nothing I can do to really change him? Ah, do not despair. Read on.

NOTES

1. Lola B. Walters, "The Grapefruit Syndrome," *Ensign,* April 1993, 13; used by permission.

2. Lecture given at Campus Education Week, Brigham Young University, August 21, 2001.

3. Neal A. Maxwell, *The Neal A. Maxwell Quote Book,* ed. Cory H. Maxwell (Salt Lake City: Bookcraft, 1997), 206.

4. Russell M. Nelson, "Our Sacred Duty to Honor Women," *Ensign,* May 1999, 39.

5. James E. Faust, "A Message to My Granddaughters: Becoming 'Great Women,'" *Ensign,* September 1986, 19–20.

6. Hugh W. Pinnock, "Making a Marriage Work," *Ensign,* September 1981, 33.

7. Gordon B. Hinckley, *Standing for Something* (New York: Times Books, 2000), 157.

8. Brent A. Barlow, *Dealing with Differences in Marriage* (Salt Lake City: Deseret Book, 1993).

9. Hinckley, *Standing for Something,* 161; emphasis added.

CHAPTER 6

No, *Really,* How Can I Change Him?

*What if every morning, you began by looking at him
and saying to yourself, "He is a wonderful man of God."
How would you treat him all day?*

I know that some of you are feeling a bit frustrated after the previous chapter. You're thinking, "Oh great, I'm supposed to let the small stuff go and understand that some of his differences complement my own. I'm supposed to do my 'guy' homework and then let him own all his problems. Lovely. But he's *still* walking around with some glaring weirdnesses that are driving me bonkers!" Do not despair, more help is on the way.

We can thoroughly understand these wonderful principles and yet still be driven batty by the consequences. Problem ownership can seem particularly thorny. We know he's got those problems. And we know just how he can fix them and how fast, and we sure wish he'd get right down to it. And yet, intellectually we understand that it really is best to control ourselves and not try to assume ownership of his problems.

So what can we do to avoid going insane? This chapter will deal with some communication skills and tools that should help.

Communication Skills—I-Messages

Let's set this up. You are practically the perfect wife. Your somewhat-imperfect husband has a problem. It's impacting you big time, and he seems oblivious. What to do? We could anesthetize ourselves with large amounts of chocolate (the staff of life for some) or we could try to learn something to help.

So often we think, "Well, if he loved me, he would *know* how I feel!" This line of reasoning is absurd. News flash: Your husband is not a psychic! So the sooner you can figure out that love has nothing to do with knowing psychically all the complex inner workings of your brain, the better off you'll be. You'll need to actually *tell* him how you feel.

When his behavior is having a negative effect on your life and your feelings, you can and should still communicate to him that you are being affected. The best way—let me rephrase that—the *only* successful way to communicate this situation is through the use of "I-messages."

I was first introduced to "I-messages" in a Church parenting class. The class was based on the book *Parent Effectiveness Training* by Dr. Thomas Gordon.[1] My husband and I took this class when our first child was a baby. It helped our parenting greatly over the years, but it totally *saved* our marriage and helped to make it great. For a complete review of the principles of problem ownership, I-messages, active listening, and negotiating, I highly recommend reading, *PET in Action* by Dr. Gordon.[2] This takes Parent Effectiveness Training and applies it to real-life examples.

So how do I-messages work? Here is the structure of an I-message:

You say, "I feel *[insert emotion or feeling]* when you *[describe behavior]* because *[impact on you]*."

Now let me emphasize the elements. You begin with the

word "I." This is about the most crucial element. If you begin your comment with the word "you" (as in "You are driving me crazy" or "You make me so mad!") you will always—repeat *always*—get exactly the same response—*shields up!* His brain and nervous system will immediately scream, *"Incoming!"* and will brace for impact. To protect himself from the onslaught that is following that word, he will instantly go into a "shields up" defensive posture. And as quickly as he is mentally able, he will push his mental "mute" button to dampen the attack. As you softly and yet firmly begin with the word "I," he will not react the same way.

The next element is to state the emotion or feeling you're experiencing. "I feel hurt . . . " or "I feel disgusted . . . " or "I feel frustrated. . . . " Try to get to the true emotion. Anger is usually a secondary emotion so you should extremely rarely say you are angry or mad. Pause and think what you are really feeling. So when he comes home very late without calling you, you could say you're feeling angry, but truly, you're probably feeling scared first. Go with that primary emotion. The truer the emotion, the more it will ring true with him.

Next, you must describe his behavior. Try to be specific. Try to avoid words like "always" or "every time" or "never," because these are exaggerations. I know, I'm really good at exaggerating. But avoid it. Instead, specifically describe the behavior in a rather flat, unemotional way: " . . . when you don't call me if you're going to be late" or " . . . when you leave your dirty underwear all over the floor." This is much better than " . . . when you never, ever call me," because he'll immediately defend himself and remind you of July 10, 1994, when he did in fact call to say he was going to be late. But don't generalize or soften it. Call a spade a spade. "I feel disgusted when you look at filthy pornography on our computer in our family room." Don't pussyfoot around and say "girlie magazines" or "your friend" when his friend is really a "mean and nasty alcoholic." Don't exaggerate but don't soften. I know it's a bit of a tightrope. You'll figure it out with practice.

Then we get to the tricky part. You next describe how the behavior is affecting you. Here again, don't exaggerate and don't soften. "I feel frustrated when you leave your dirty underwear on the floor because I have to pick it up so the room looks nice." "I feel hurt when you comment on the appearance of other women when we're at the beach because it makes me feel inferior." "I'm scared when you are late getting to work because you could get fired and we'd have no income and could lose the house."

This part, talking about how you are affected, is absolutely required. And it will also be a good guide for you. If you cannot come up with a concrete way in which you're being affected, you're obviously trying to own *his* problem. So don't say anything. He's left to own the problem and fix it for himself. Think about it. How does his messy desk at work really affect you? How does his performance on his Church job affect you? You cannot resort to saying you're embarrassed over everything. Women tend to feel embarrassed simply because their husbands are less than perfect. Not going to fly, ladies. You can't resort to that one.

Obviously, it is best if you practice these ahead of time so they flow and you're not sitting there going, "Uh, uh . . . let's see, what's your behavior . . . ?" and he's left wondering what in the world you're trying now.

What's interesting is that when you begin to use this, you will often get one reaction. He'll say, "Gee, I had no idea you felt that way! What can I do to help you?" He may genuinely have had no idea how his actions were troubling you or may not have tuned into realizing how much they were affecting you. At this point, you'll think, "Man, why didn't I tell him this sooner?" or you'll realize that you did tell him, but you told him in a way that he didn't connect the dots and truly hear you.

Now I'd like to review some helpful techniques in using this communication skill. After you've made your statement *do not*, I repeat, *do not* say, "So you should . . . " Ah, the dreaded "you" word. What happens when you move into that mode? Shields up! Hit the mute button! You had him for a little while, but then he heard that incoming wife-missile and pulled his head into his shell. So bite your tongue at the end of the I-message. Clamp it down. Do not give him a list of things he needs to do to fix the problem. You are merely stating how it affects you. *He* is responsible for fixing it.

Some women will say, "Well, can we make suggestions?" Oh, sneaky, sneaky women. I say, "no!" and they're a bit flustered. "Well, what if he asks for suggestions?" I chuckle a bit over this. They just can't stand it. Let him fix it? On his own? Oh, it makes us so vulnerable. And we all know exactly how to fix his problems, don't we? Resist all of these urges. Walk away if you feel them coming on. As you grow very adept at using I-messages (in other words, after you've been doing it for a decade or so), you might (that's *might)* be able to handle giving a few suggestions. But be careful. It is too easy to slip back into owning his problems and running his life. It's a slippery slope. So while you're beginning, do *not* give out suggestions, hints, pointers, or whatever you would like to rationalize and call them.

In fact, it is best to make these statements very short and succinct. Wives have a tendency to go on and on and on. (One of my favorite comments from my son: "Don't your lips ever stop moving?" I laughed so hard I almost lost it.) So remember KISS—Keep It Short and Simple! This has a funny result. He'll be surprised. He'll be braced for impact. He'll just know that the harangue is coming. He'll have his finger just hovering over the "mute" button. So shock the bejeebers out of him and just walk away. If he asks you for clarification, repeat your statement clearly. And then say, "That's it. I just wanted you to know." Turn and walk away again. He'll be stunned. And he'll be thinking.

Remember to focus on "I." He cannot argue with how you feel or how you are affected. He may try. He may say, "Well, that's stupid." Or, "You shouldn't feel that way." Or, "You are always so emotional. You overreact." Again, be firm. Repeat your statement if you feel it's appropriate, and then walk away. Most husbands will then have to face how their behavior is affecting you negatively, and they'll feel very uncomfortable or sad about it. Let that just sit with them. Let them just face it and think about it.

Now whether or not he chooses to fix it will depend on where he is and where the marriage and love are. It may be something very simple, and he may be willing to try to fix it. When he does, be sure to notice even his small efforts. It may be something big, something he just can't handle right now. Be clear on how it's affecting you, and then you can decide if you're willing to give him the time and space to fix it. Most of the time, he will try. And he cannot deny or try to keep his head in the sand about how his behavior is affecting others. Call it a mini-intervention, if you will.

As I said, most of the time, a husband will face it and try to fix it. "Oh, I didn't realize that hurt your feelings. I'll call you every day when I leave work so you know when I'm coming home for dinner." And he'll give it his best shot. Thank him when he does. Use I-statements in a positive way. "I feel so loved when you call me from work. Thank you!"

He may try to stall. "Well, I always forget to pick up my socks. You know I'm not good at that kind of thing." Don't appease. Let him own it. Repeat. And every time he plops his socks down, he'll think, "Gee, this really bothers her. It is pretty stupid." And hopefully, eventually, he'll take that extra one second to huck them into the hamper. And he'll know that he made you happy. And he'll feel proud of himself that he solved a problem.

Let's face it. Most men just *love* to solve problems. So let your husband do so. He'll feel better about himself because he'll understand how you feel and be able to fix it. He'll be grateful for a smart wife who lets him know how she feels. He'll appreciate the fact that you don't attack him and tell him how to solve issues. It is a powerful communication skill. It will get easier with practice, so just give it a try and keep at it.

"Treat As If" Principle

Now if I could isolate one thing in this entire book that is worth remembering, this is it. So wake up and pay attention!

Let me set this up a bit for you. In 1976 I was at BYU as a freshman, and I was there a week early for a conference. I was walking through the student activity center when I noticed a large class going on. You need to know that I was in the throes of homesickness on a major scale. I did not handle new situations very well (the understatement of the century) and was basically a weeping mess. So I see this class and I sit down in the back to listen. It happened to be BYU Education Week. I, a young girl from Detroit, didn't know what that was and I probably owe someone $20 for sitting in that class. The speaker was teaching a principle to the class that he called the Act As If Principle. You may have heard of it.

In a nutshell, the Act As If Principle means that you act or pretend as if you have a certain attribute and eventually you will. He had a person come up to the stage and told him to walk across the stage as if they had very low self-esteem. The young man slouched across the stage staring at the floor. He asked the audience, "How likely are you to talk to this person or think they're a fun person to get to know?" Of course, everyone answered in the negative. Then he had the young man act as if he were very popular and confident. The boy strutted across the stage with a big confident smile, shoulders up, and waved to everyone. The instructor asked the audience, "Now how likely would you be to say hello and interact with him?" Everyone answered in the positive. He continued, "But it's the same guy. Why would you say hello now and not before?" The answer was obvious. Then he asked an important question, "Which one represents who he really is?" None of us had a clue because we didn't know him. "Precisely," the teacher replied. "And yet, if he *acted* as if he were confident, you would react as if he were confident."

Well, let's just say it was one of those "Aha!" moments in my life. I cannot begin to tell you what a transformation of understanding occurred in that hard little chair in the back of the ballroom. I realized that I had the power to change my life. I had been acting as the most unconfident young woman there was. So I went over to the bathroom in the Jesse Knight Building (I can still even remember the stall!) and cried my brains out and thanked the Lord for opening my eyes to a way to change. And from that day on, I acted as if I were confident. I really pretended hard. And in three days, I, who had had hardly even one date in my life, had a marriage proposal. Okay, I was converted to the power of the Act As If Principle. (No, I didn't marry the guy— are you crazy? Who would propose in three days?) I have used this principle to change from being an extremely shy wallflower to being comfortable in front of hundreds giving a speech.

One day I was pondering this principle because I was preparing my lectures on Being the Perfect Wife for Education Week that year. (Full circle, eh? I was transformed and now I teach others.) It was Sunday morning, and I was drying my hair. I do a lot of thinking while I dry my hair. I was thinking, "So I truly, *deeply* believe in this principle. But how do you get your husband to 'Act As If'?" At that moment, it was like my head opened up and this understanding was downloaded into my brain.

I learned the Treat As If Principle. It is this: "If you will treat your husband as if he possesses a certain attribute, over time he will begin to *act* as if he possesses that attribute. Eventually, that will become *who he is*." Reread that several times until it sinks in your head. In a moment, I received such an understanding of the power and truth of this principle that it is difficult to convey it in words.

If you would like your husband to be a patient man, treat him as if he is a patient man. All of your interactions will be based on this: you believe that he is a patient man (yes, you're pretending, but do it anyway). You will not jump to conclusions. You will not scold him when he isn't. In fact, you'll be pretending so hard you'll say to yourself, "I know that he is a patient man. He just slipped this time." Think about it. Every time, every single time, you interact, you will treat him as if he's patient. Guess what will happen over time? He will act more and more that way. And as he does, you will notice it and comment on it and reinforce it. Eventually, he will become a patient man.

The biggest key to using this principle is to absolutely and completely be *relentless* in treating him "as if." Let me repeat that word so you don't forget it—you must be **relentless**. If you treat him "as if" some of the time and then revert to treating him as if he's *not*, he will not change. He will comfortably revert to his previous behavior. So you cannot give up and you cannot give in. You must pretend and treat him "as if" so thoroughly and so profoundly that you begin to believe it in your heart as well.

An interesting thing happens sometimes as you do this. I tried the patient one first myself. I think my hubby had blown up at the kids that day or something. I thought, "I'm going to give this a try!" So for two weeks, I relentlessly treated my husband as if he were a patient man. And after two weeks I stopped and thought, "You know what, he really is a patient guy already!" As I began to really tune into this and notice his behavior, I came to the dawning realization that he was already very patient. Okay, so I'm a little slow sometimes. But I had been focusing on those very rare instances when he had not been patient. (Can't imagine him acting that way in a home where we had four sons and a very hyper wife!) So sometimes as you begin to treat him as if, you will discover that he already is.

Let's run through an example to see how this works. Let's just say you've been frustrated with how your husband acts with respect to spiritual things in the home. You would like him to be a better patriarch. (Like I said, that probably just hit the vast majority of wives out there.) So you are going to treat him as if he were a wonderful patriarch in the home—a veritable spiritual giant. You are going to treat him as if he presides in your home. Okay, so it's time for family prayer. As the family is gathered, you bow your head and keep your mouth shut. The patriarch in the home calls on the person to give prayer, right? After some uncomfortable moments of quiet (where everyone is peeking at each other wondering what is wrong with mother), your husband will say, "Uh, honey, weren't you going to call on someone to say the prayer?" "Oh, no," you reply, "I realized that that was *your* job as the patriarch in the home. I'm sorry I've been messing up on that. I won't do it again." Now all the kids are rather bug-eyed and glancing at Dad. Dad squares his shoulders and says, "Uh, oh, well then. Uh, Jimmy would you pray?" Never again do you take over at family prayer. And from then on, he will act as the patriarch and call on someone to pray.

It's time for family home evening. The family is gathered. You sit and wait for him to conduct. You do *not* jump in and run the show because the patriarch is the one who presides. So a similar drill ensues. And things begin to change. In fact, the next week, you comment before family home evening, "Honey, who do you think should present the lesson next week?" And that night, he then makes assignments for the next week. And over time, he begins to call the family to gather, and away he goes.

What if, every morning, you began by looking at him and saying to yourself, "He is a wonderful man of God." How would you treat him all day? If you kept that thought right there in front of your eyes, how would you act? You can see the major shift in how you would behave, can't you. And yes, for some men this is a huge leap of imagination. But you can pretend. You can relentlessly treat "as if." And over time, not only will he begin to act *as if* he is, but he will *become* that wonderful man of God. And you will believe that he is to the core of your being as well.

It's so odd that we go around wanting our hubby to be the spiritual patriarch in our home but we go around treating him as if he's not. And then we wonder why not!

Treat him as if he's romantic. Treat him as if he's kind. Treat him as if he's thoughtful. Treat him as if he's intelligent. Whatever it is you feel he might need to change, you can treat him as if he has already changed. He can become it if you will treat him that way long enough and hard enough.

Now the reverse can also be true. If you treat your husband as if he is a lazy, irresponsible man, *he might just show you you're right*. It's like self-fulfilling prophecy. I see this everywhere around me. Let me share the story of Dee. Dee was very exasperated by her husband. She thought he was the flakiest, nonpatriarchal guy on the planet. And so she treated him like that all the time. So when stake priesthood meeting was announced, she'd say, "Well, of course *you're* not going." When the subject of home teaching came up, she'd say, "Oh, he *never* does his home teaching. I don't know why they bother to assign him to any-one." She would make little "dig" comments to him and about him to others all the time. Small wonder that bit by bit he went inactive. Then she would point and say, "See, I just knew he would." I thought, "Well, of course he would! You treated him relentlessly as if he would, and so he did!" She was so caught up in this cycle that she could not see the tremendous damage she was doing. If a wife treats her husband as if he is a lazy, irrespon-sible oaf, he will be.

Now you may think that this won't work in your circum-stances. You make think, "Oh, she doesn't know my husband. He's not a kind man and he never will be." You're right. I don't know him. But I dare you to try. Give it a whole year. Just say, "Okay, I'm going to relentlessly treat him as if he's a kind man for an entire year." And no fair mentally cheating. When you think, "Yeah, well, I'm just faking it. He's really an unkind man and always will be," you stop your brain right there and make yourself repeat three times: "My husband is a kind man. The sweet man I married is a very kind man. That darling man I love is the kindest man on earth." Now you may be laughing, but it will replace those negative thoughts in your head. Go ahead, I dare you to try.

Keep in mind that we are talking only about *your* actions and *your* mindset here. You can control these. And a big part of having your actions be consistent is having your mind in sync. You can use this method of repeating positive statements in your head or whatever method works for you. But if you hope it to be truly effective and long-lasting, it is important to try to keep your actions and your mental outlook in harmony.

But remember problem ownership. Your husband (not you) is still responsible for changing his own behavior. Also, I am not suggesting in the slightest that your actions or inactions in living this principle actually cause your husband to behave in a certain way. As we discussed under the section on problem ownership, there are too many wives who believe that their husband's behavior is their (the wife's) fault, and that is simply untrue.

But I am suggesting that altering how you behave can create a climate where your husband can change, if he chooses to do so.

Understandably, agency is still in place. He may choose not to change for a while or at the pace you would like or at all. But do not ever forget. Your husband is a choice spirit reserved for the latter days. If you keep treating him "as if," his spirit will usually respond. It may indeed take time, but we're in this for eternity. If you interact with him in this positive way, it will have an impact.

And think about it for a minute. Let's say you treat him as if he were a loving man. And let's say he never ever changes one bit. And you try it for a whole year. And still no change. You may think all is lost. But not so. Take a step back and look at what happened. How have *you* changed? Ah, interesting, isn't it? Every morning you woke up and looked at him and said, "My husband is a loving man." And all day you behaved that way. How do you feel about yourself and your behavior? I dare say that treating "as if" felt a whole lot better to you and made you a whole lot better. So even if he doesn't change or if his change is glacial, it will still bless your marriage and bless you as you behave in a more Christlike fashion.

This works on children as well. As our son approached the age of fourteen, we would make comments like, "Well, here it comes. All boys turn squirrelly at age fourteen. This is going to be tough." And guess what, like a self-fulfilling prophecy Connor turned fourteen and almost drove us nuts. When he turned fifteen, he improved. We did the same thing with our second son and again, he was crazy at fourteen and calmer at fifteen. So not to be totally dense, we realized that we had been thinking and acting "as if" in a negative way and took a new approach with the next two boys. We would say, "Gee, boys are sure rascals at age eight, aren't they? We love it when they turn fourteen because they act so mature." (This was after they were long past eight.) It's weird but it worked. The last two sailed through age fourteen with much less of the weirdness that does naturally occur at that age. Just don't tell them that we all know that fourteen is a high-mutant age. We were pretending and it helped greatly!

Once you understand this principle clearly, you will see that the Lord uses it a lot. Think of the temple ordinances. Virtually all of the temple ordinances treat you as if you are a queen and a goddess. Go to the temple and go through all the ordinances, not just the endowment. It will amaze you at how the Lord takes this approach over and over. The Lord repeatedly teaches you that you are blessed, that you have power, that you can become like God—indeed, that it is your destiny. You can't help but come out of there an improved and changed person. I believe that is one reason we are encouraged to go to the temple often. We are treated as if we are already celestial. Once we get home, we act much better and the impact of that "treat as if" lesson lingers throughout the week.

I cannot overemphasize the power of the Treat As If Principle. It can transform you as a wife, and it can transform your marriage. It is certainly worth the effort.

Faith, Hope, Charity— Mormon's Good Advice for Wives

One day I was reading Mormon's words as recorded in Moroni 7 and realized that the entire chapter related clearly to being the perfect wife. That caused me to look at Mormon's counsel in a whole different way. Mormon talks about faith, hope, and charity and the importance of having each. Each of these principles applies to being a great wife.

Faith—have faith in your husband. The truth of the matter is that he's probably a good man who is trying to do his best. Every day when he gets up, he tries. There is probably not one day that he wakes up and announces, "Today I will be a lousy husband!" Never happens. So because you believe in him, have faith in him. Tell him you have faith in him. As we went through extended unemployment, I would often say, "Honey, I have total faith in you. I know that you will take care of our family." That's a different message from "I sure love you!" It's empowering on a whole different level.

And sometimes when you are feeling doubtful, take a step back. Remember all the great things he has done. Tell yourself, "I absolutely have faith in him." I find that it even does a world of good to me. It changes my perception. After I say that to myself, I often think, "You know what? You're right. I *do* have faith in him! I've seen him handle so much. He can handle this." It instills confidence in my heart as well.

You also can treat him "as if" you have faith in him. And he will respond well to that vote of confidence. It will help him have the self-confidence and empowerment to succeed. One of the truly great roles a wife plays in the life of her husband is cheerleader. Everyone needs a cheerleader, and you're it for him. Give him that great gift.

I think of Jeannette when I think of this principle. Jeannette married young, and we were all a bit concerned because her husband was perceived as, well, not being a great prize pick. But Jeannette thought the sun rose and set with this guy. She always acted and spoke as if she had total faith in her husband. And it was amazing to watch what unfolded. She had complete faith that he would be active in the Church, and so he was. She had complete faith that he would be steady in his job and provide for the family, and so he did. I've watched the months and years go by, and I've watched this man bloom under the gaze of a wife who had complete faith in his ability to do well. It was nothing short of miraculous. And I was rather humbled to see how completely she radiated this faithfulness. It taught me much.

The opposite is also true. If you don't have faith in him, he will absolutely know it. It will be the most painful hurt he will feel. The repercussions of that behavior will be devastating. So pretend if you have to for a while.

Remember to express your faith often to your husband. It will be like sunshine to a flower. Mormon stated, "For it is by faith that miracles are wrought" (Moroni 7:37). Those miracles can occur in your own marriage and with your own husband. He will bask in your faith in him and be a better man for it.

Mormon also taught that hope is crucial. Of course he was talking about hope through the atonement, but those same precepts apply to hope in your marriage. He said, "Wherefore, if a [wo]man have faith [s]he must needs have hope; for without faith there cannot be any hope" (Moroni 7:42; verse changed to reflect a woman's perspective). Hope plays an important part in marriage. Hold on to every hope that your marriage will develop into an excellent one. Keep your hope in the growth of both your husband and yourself alive and well. Feed it. Again, self-talk is so helpful here. Keep positive statements in your head, and they will fan the flame of that hope in your heart. I have seen women buckle down in very difficult times and cling to that hope in a situation others would have perceived as hopeless. And their hope and faith have been rewarded.

Finally, Mormon counsels us to have charity, explaining that "charity is the pure love of Christ, and it endureth forever" (Moroni 7:47). The most important thing you can do is to treat your husband with that pure love, with true charity. It is the one thing he wants from you the most. He wants your love. He wants your love more than anything else you can give him.

A wife discussing the difficulty she faced in her marriage said, "The struggles we coped with were draining. Pressures stemming from our son's illness were pulling us apart. I wanted to spend most of my time with my small son while my husband buried himself in activity—anything to keep busy. I thought he was indifferent; he thought I was hovering too much over our son. We fought almost daily. I was miserable and didn't think our marriage could last.

"Then I felt the hand of Heavenly Father guide me, through a friend, to hear a talk about charity in marriage. The speaker suggested being charitable toward your spouse for just one month. I knew it would never work with *my* husband! But because I wasn't going to let it be my fault if we got a divorce, I determined to stop nagging and fighting with my husband for the next four weeks, which I did.

"I turned to the scriptures and read about charity in Moroni 7. I learned that charity belongs more in marriage than anywhere else. As I changed, my husband began to change too. After the month was over, my husband was a different person!

"Those weeks marked the beginning of a journey toward better times."[3]

Again, this pure love is something that must be fed in order to survive. How can you feed it? A positive outlook can help significantly—focus on and remember all those things you love about your husband. It helps tremendously to keep that voice in your head that talks constantly in a positive frame of reference toward your husband.

One day I was particularly annoyed at my husband. I have no idea what it was about, but I'm sure that it was very serious and extremely dramatic. At least that's the story I'm sticking with at this point. So I went on a walk. Those long walks are so therapeutic! I think I've saved a lot of therapy costs by going on that hour-long walk so often. So I'm walking along thinking, "Dagnabbit!" (yes, I do say "dagnabbit" to myself). I'm thinking, "That Steve. He ticks me off so much. I don't know. You'd think after twenty-five years of marriage he would be much further along and I wouldn't have to deal with all of this hooey." (I use rather colorful language when conversing with myself.) Now before the little devil on my shoulder completely overwhelmed me, the little angel on the other side piped up. "Now, Merrilee, you know that he's not that bad. Why don't you give a thankful prayer right now?"

I have found that a well-timed "thankful prayer" can change my perspective instantly. So I began to pray. "Father, I thank thee for my Stevie. He is a good man. I'm thankful that he's toughed it out with me because I could drive a normal man batty. I'm thankful that he's such a wonderful father. I'm thankful that he thinks I'm pretty. I'm thankful that he likes *Star Trek* and *Star Wars*. [I didn't say this had to be particularly deep.] I'm thankful that he has beautiful eyes. I'm thankful that he likes to camp. I'm thankful that he gives me flowers on Mother's Day. I'm thankful that he goes to church every week. I'm thankful that he took me to the temple." On and on it went for about forty-five minutes. (I'm sure that the drivers in Poway think their city councilwoman is a wacky nut job because I'm always talking when I'm walking.) You can imagine, now that you've gotten to know me some, what I was at this point. You got it! I was a weeping mess! I was crying my eyes out. I couldn't wait to run back home and tell my sweetie how much I loved and adored him.

When you feel that charity waning, try making a positive list. Include every little thing you can think of and every sweet memory. It will work wonders. Even when you're really, really mad. It can give you perspective.

Notice the power of having charity: "Charity suffereth long, and is kind, and envieth not, and is not puffed up, seeketh not her own, is not easily provoked, thinketh no evil, and rejoiceth not in iniquity but rejoiceth in the truth, beareth all things, believeth all things, hopeth all things, endureth all things. . . . Charity never faileth" (Moroni 7:45–46).

Oh what good advice for the smart wife! The smart wife suffereth long. She hangeth in there for decades.

And she is kind. Of all the sweet things a man cherishes in his wife, kindness is way up there. Just simply being kind in what we say and in what we do can make a great difference. Every husband wants to come home to a kind woman—not a shrew. Listen to how beautifully the Lord puts it when he tells wives what they are to do: "The office of thy calling shall be for a comfort unto . . . thy husband, in his afflictions, with consoling words, in the spirit of meekness" (D&C 25:5). It is a kind woman who can comfort her husband. That's the kind of wife he is eager to come home to.

When we have charity, we "envieth not" the computer or all the time he's spending on his Church calling or the time he spends helping his parents or the fact that he gets to eat really nice lunches and we're at home with the kids eating tuna fish.

"Is not puffed up" really describes the danger so many women find themselves in. We're seeing an entire generation of "puffed up" women who think men are worthless. Let's choose not to go there.

He continues: "charity . . . seeketh not her own." Note the female pronoun. He could have said, "Okay, wives, I'm really talking to you at this point." He didn't—but we get it. "Seeketh not her own" way all the time so that the husband never ever gets his way. "Seeketh not her own" agenda so that he's blindsided every time they have a conversation because she's got her hidden agenda lurking in the wings to pounce upon.

"Is not easily provoked." Oh, my. Okay, that one hits close to home, doesn't it! Sometimes some of us are *so* easily provoked. We tend to be emotional and take things personally. Also, we get to deal with rampant and swinging hormones, and that adds to our degree of difficulty on this one. Our first step is to be aware, and our second step is to tone down our reactions. But a wife operating with charity cuts her husband some slack and doesn't fly off the handle at every little thing, which is something we can probably all work on in our quest for smart wifeness.

"Thinketh no evil, and rejoiceth not in iniquity but rejoiceth in the truth" is good advice for a woman who is trying to have faith in her husband. Many women are extremely suspicious types. Just today on the radio a woman was jumping to the conclusion that her husband was having an affair. The host of the program asked if her husband had ever given her any reason to doubt him. The wife stated that he had not. She was advised to trust him. Sometimes we jump to conclusions and think evil of our husbands. If this is a tendency of ours, it needs to be nipped in the bud. I like that it says, "rejoiceth in the truth." So often we go around wondering and wondering and don't take the time to ask. Get to the truth. Just ask the question—flat out. Then you can deal with the truth and not fret about the unknown any longer.

A charitable wife "beareth all things." She putteth up with his love of sports. She beareth all his children and beareth his different parenting style. She hangeth in there when he hates ballet and loves repairing cars on the driveway. She beareth his differences with a patient smile and a charitable heart. A smart wife does a lot of bearething!

She "believeth all things" and always gives him the benefit of the doubt. She "hopeth all things" will work out well, and keepeth that hope aflameth in her heart. (Yes, I'm having fun with this.)

Finally, she "endureth all things." She endures them as long as it takes. And why does she do all of this?

Because "charity never faileth." That pure love she has for her husband *never, ever, EVER* fails. And if she can hang on to that charity, miracles will happen and her marriage will last in charity for an eternity. Truly the blessing we all seek.

Don't we all want our husbands to love us this way? To look on all our foibles and weaknesses with a charitable and patient heart? Let's give him this great gift. And it will be returned to us. The great thing about charity is that it grows when used.

Give It Time and Prayer

When you have tried absolutely everything you can think of to fix your husband and have totally run out of options, consider simply giving it time and prayer. It is amazing what simple time will do.

Consider the cycles of a typical marriage. The first year is honeymoon when he looked so good and you looked so good and he was so perfect and you were, of course, perfect as well. Ah, that blissful first year! Then years two through four are reality check time. You realize he has some disturbing habits that you thought were cute but are now simply annoying. I call this the "Oh-my-goodness-what-have-I-done?" phase. Some deep soul-searching goes on as you realize that this is permanent and maybe he's not quite so perfect after all. (Of course, you are still perfect, so no worries there.)

And so you spend years five through ten working out the kinks. There is a lot of adjusting going on during this time. That's why seven years sees the highest divorce rate. Some couples realize that those kinks just aren't going to work out and they bail out. Lots of marital work goes on during these years because you're often having children, setting up house, and establishing a career for the provider, and things are shifting and changing.

Ten years of marriage is a great landmark. You often have reached a compromise on most issues, and things are usually fairly okay. Lots of the major stuff has been worked out. The companionship is solidifying. And you're still looking pretty good and he's looking pretty good.

From years twenty and up, you have to be careful if things get a little too smooth sailing. You look okay and he looks okay. Sometimes we need a little intensity to spice things up a bit. Be aware of staleness during this time period.

By fifty years, you figure that the whole intensity thing is overrated, and it looks likely that you'll stay together. You don't really care how you look and think his bald head is kind of cute. And you can't imagine life without him.

So be aware of the impact of time on your marriage and on you as a wife. Sometimes the problems and concerns you have about your marriage and your husband are cyclical. Often they just reflect the normal adjusting that takes place.

Take a look at some of those remaining issues of concern in your marriage. Pick out the ones that really aren't that big of a deal or that you will give your spouse some time to work on. And then put them on the shelf. Say to yourself, "If this still bothers me in five years, I'll address the issue." That may sound like a radical solution. But remember, you've tried everything else and it's still there. So why not give it some time and see if that solves it? We're in this for the long haul, right?

Often problems will dissipate and go away completely. Or we may get used to things, and frankly, we often don't really care anymore. When you step back and look at things years later, you will probably think, "Gee, what was I so upset about?"

Here's a funny example. I couldn't stand my husband's nose. I mean, his nose is perfect. Way too perfect. It's like totally and precisely straight. Bugged me to death. I thought noses should have some "character," as mine did. I'd worn glasses forever so my nose had some, well, shape to it as you went down that bridge line. His could have been constructed by a laser, it was so straight and perfect. So this bothered me. I know, I know. It was weird. But for the first two years of our marriage it drove me crazy. Finally, I thought, "Okay, Merrilee, this is not something you are going to be able to change. Why don't you quit obsessing over this and put it on a shelf for a while?" I did. When I'd think about it, I'd nip it and remind myself that it was assigned to the shelf.

Well, now I look at his nose and I think, "How nice! How handsome he is!" And I think that I was so incredibly weird and obsessive and must have had serious mental problems. With age has come perspective, and I realize that this was totally absurd and inconsequential and that many other things are more important. True story.

So put some of your concerns on that shelf and let them sit a while. As my wise sister counseled me once, "Merrilee, aren't you in this for an eternity? Why not give it some time?" Good advice then and good advice now. Just give it some time.

Of course, we could not survive doing this without prayer. So while those items are sitting on the shelf, feel free to add them to your prayers. The one thing that will help is to pray specifically about them. So often we just ask the Lord to "Please bless my husband." The more specific we can be, the better we'll be able to draw on the powers of heaven for our spouse. Also, I believe that we will be prompted more specifically on ways we can help or handle those issues.

By now I'm sure that we have handled all of his faults, and that you have learned a lot about how to change your husband (or not to, I daresay!).

Remember, your attitude is a big part of the solution. Sister

Wendy Watson gave beautiful advice to wives: "What happens when a wife fervently prays, 'Please help me to love my husband as the Savior loves him. Help me to see all that is good about him'? . . . And perhaps there are times when the most effectual prayer of each spouse needs to be, 'Please help me to see this situation from my spouse's point of view.' Eyes that see things through a lens of love can see so much more clearly."[4]

May each of us reach a new understanding of our husbands. May we have the patience to let them solve their own problems. May we have the clarity to have our voices heard. And may we treat our husbands with dignity and respect and charity so that we can watch them rise up to become true sons of God. And I hope that each of us will treat them as if they already are.

NOTES

1. Thomas Gordon, *Parent Effectiveness Training* (New York: Three Rivers Press, 2000). See chapter 7.

2. Thomas Gordon, *P.E.T. in Action* (New York: Bantam, 1984).

3. "Mending Our Marriage," *Ensign,* October 1996, 49.

4. Wendy L. Watson, *Purity and Passion* (Salt Lake City: Deseret Book, 2001), 22–23.

How to Be a Fun-*Living* Wife

The second most important thing you'll learn in this book is this: you have to keep dating only the husband you want to keep.

Well, now that we've raked our husbands over the coals, let's turn our attention back to perfecting ourselves. By now, you've totally mastered all the do's and don'ts. You're looking positively fabulous, feeling brilliant and deeply profound as you nourished body, mind, and spirit. And you've got your husband whipped into shape.

It's time to have fun!

Remember, a boring wife is . . . a boring wife!

We're going to talk about how to be a fun-*living* wife. There's a vast difference between a fun-loving wife and a fun-*living* one. A fun-loving wife sits on the beach and says, "Oh, look at them playing in the waves!" Or sits in the house while the family swims saying, "I don't want to mess up my hair." A fun-*living* wife hits the waves with a boogie board!

I'm not going to be delving into sexual intimacy in this chapter. I figure there are plenty of books that talk about that subject and if you are having concerns there, I would suggest you read some. Enough said.

So let's do a test to see if you need to read this chapter.

Top Ten Clues That You Are a Boring Wife

1. The last treat you bought for your husband was a big roll of garbage bags.
2. You don't have any girlfriends, really, unless you count your visiting teacher.
3. Your bathing suit is at least a decade old and the elastic is shot.
4. You tell your husband you love him once a year on New Year's Eve.
5. Your idea of a good time is to clip coupons.
6. Your idea of a fun date with your husband is to cruise the aisles at Wal-Mart.
7. You quit flirting because, by gum, ya'll got yer man!
8. The last time you went on a date with your husband was in the last millennium.
9. The last time you went on an overnighter with just you and your husband was to attend a funeral.
10. The only reason you're still reading this book is that you're stuck at the orthodontist with the children and you've already read all of their magazines!

Oh dear, I can see that we have some work to do! Well, let's get right to it.

President Kimball counseled, "Many couples permit their marriages to become stale and their love to grow cold like old bread or worn-out jokes or cold gravy. . . . These people will do well to reevaluate, to renew their courting, to express their affection, to acknowledge kindnesses, and to increase their consideration so their marriage again can become beautiful, sweet, and growing." And he promises couples in the Church: "While marriage is difficult, and discordant and frustrated marriages are common, yet real, lasting happiness is possible, and marriage can be more an exultant ecstasy than the human mind can conceive."[1]   *This takes Faith & Work*

His counsel is well taken, and we need to give special attention to bringing fun and joy back into our marriage relationship. So let's talk about some ideas that will help.

Here's a good beginning place—the second most important thing you'll learn in this book is this: you have to keep dating only the husband you want to keep.

Date Night—The Key to Having Fun and Helping Your Marriage Survive

My parents gave me a great legacy. They faithfully dated. They were married over sixty years and dated up until the last couple of weeks of my dad's life. What a great example they set! As a result, it was always drilled into me both by my parents and my older sister that you must date your husband—every single week.

This was absolutely the number 1 best thing I did to improve my marriage. You want to be a fun-living wife? I recommend dating weekly.

Now I can just hear the litany of lame excuses you're coming up with, so let's just get them out of the way.

Lame Excuse 1—"We don't have enough time."

Do you hear what you're saying? Your number 1 eternal relationship and you don't have time? Really? You don't have enough time for your husband? Oh, so you're *really, really* busy. What was I thinking? (Yes, that is sarcasm dripping.) As I've asked before, didn't you get the bonus three hours that the rest of us got? (I know, more sarcasm.) Okay, look at this excuse with eyes wide open. This tells where your priorities are. We all have the same time. So you're saying I *choose* not to devote my time to this. That is the real nugget of truth.

This excuse has now been declared *lame* and no longer works.

Lame Excuse 2—"He won't go."

I know that you're perfectly willing and able and that he's the holdout, right?

Let me just share another story here. Steve and I dated faithfully after we got married. And then we had our first son and it was a difficult time with his career, and for some reason we fell out of the habit. After about three months, I was going stir-crazy and realized that we had let this slip. So I said to Stevie, "Honey, let's go out on a date this week."

And he said, "Well, I don't know."

I responded, "Well, let me rephrase that. I am going to hire a sitter on Friday night at 6:00 P.M. I will then be going out to have some fun. I would love for you to join me." Steve was very noncommittal.

So Friday night rolls around and I go and get the sitter. I'm all dressed up and come in with the sitter and Steve's sitting there. I said, "Uh, honey, I have the sitter. Are you ready to go?"

He said, "I don't feel like it."

I said, "Well, uh, okay. I'm going anyway." I instructed the sitter on how to care for our perfect little son and away I went. Steve holed up in the den with his computer with the door shut. Now at this point, I'm sure the sitter was tempted to call home and ask her parents if there were any mental problems in the Boyack family but I'm not sure she did. I'm sure she was wondering.

So out I went. I went out to dinner. Went shopping. Had a great time. And back I came and drove the sitter home. She, bless her heart, didn't say a thing. And I didn't say a thing to Steve. After a while, he asked, "So what did you do?"

I replied, "Oh, I had a great time. Went out to dinner at that restaurant we like. Did a little shopping. It was great." He just mumbled a reply.

So the next week comes and I give him a heads up that Friday is looming. He is again quite noncommittal. I get dressed up and go get the sitter. We come back. And he announces *again* that he is not interested in going. (Can you believe it?) I said, "Well, that's fine. I'm heading out." So I'm sure at this point that the baby-sitter is dialing the bishop to inquire if the Boyacks are in the midst of severe marital problems. Steve sequesters himself in his office and away I go. (Now, looking back on this, that was probably not a good idea. I'm not sure I would have been happy with my kid baby-sitting when the weird husband was locked in the den. Not that Steve is the slightest bit weird, but you have to admit that this was very odd. Anyway, I digress.) So off I go to dinner and a show this time. Come back, drive sitter home, and say nothing. Steve asks, "So what did you do tonight?" I tell him I had a great time—good food, great movie. At no point do I complain that he is not accompanying me on these adventures.

Next week comes. I get the sitter. And Steve is ready to go out. (Much to the relief of the poor sitter, I am sure.)

And we've hardly missed a week since.

✳So if your husband refuses to go, get creative. Maybe your mother could come over and watch your kids. That *might* work.

Again, this excuse is declared officially *lame*.

Lame Excuse 3—"We're broke!"

Good try on this one. But sorry, it just doesn't fly either. Dates can be free. I repeat, dates can be free.

Let me list ten date nights that cost nothing:

1. Go on a walk in the park or on the beach and hold hands and talk.
2. Take a blanket to the mountains or wherever and look up at the stars and describe what it would be like to live on another planet.
3. Go to Costco and eat the free samples and then watch a DVD on your laptop computer in your car facing the sunset. (Fun to make out too. Oh, I am SO not going there!)
4. Go on a bike ride.
5. Take a free class offered in the community. (There are lots of them.)
6. Go to the bookstore and read love poems to each other.
7. Take your iPod or boombox or whatever to a remote parking lot and dance together in the beams of your car's headlights.
8. Walk through a crowded area and make up stories about other people's lives. Be creative! Be funny!
9. Go skating, surfing, boogie-boarding, swimming, hiking, backpacking, or whatever sport you like.
10. Go to a cemetery and look at the cool headstones or go to the airport and watch planes land or to the port and watch boats dock.

There are books that are published on this topic for poor, starving college students. I know because I bought one for my son. So if you're poor and starving, by all means, check them out.

Creativity will totally remedy this excuse. Now I know that sometimes baby-sitting costs can be an issue. We had no family nearby and I swear we put half the neighborhood and ward through college. If you have family members and you're broke, beg them for a couple of hours each week. Or even better, trade with other, similarly situated families. They can watch yours on Friday, and you can watch theirs on Saturday.

Remember, dating is cheaper than therapy! It just needs to be your priority. Barbara Workman talks about learning this lesson: "We couldn't understand Larry and his new wife. Medical school shouldn't allow time to play tennis so frequently, but that's what they were doing—and they were even going on vacations! Being a few years older and wiser, we knew life was too serious for the amount of time they were spending just enjoying each other. But for twenty years now we've watched that marriage continue with the same exhilaration, and we love to be with them because we know there will be smiles and laughter.

"Larry explained his philosophy to us soon after we met him: 'Our marriage is an eternal relationship. If it is strong and happy, then I can live with whatever challenges life brings. If it isn't, then no wonderful job or anything else can make up for that loss. Our marriage is going to get the highest priority of my time, money, and energy.'"[2]

So this excuse is declared null, void, and obviously *lame*.

Dating your husband is incredibly fun. It is a great time to reconnect. My sister and her husband would announce as they were leaving, "Well, we're going out to fall in love again!" And they meant it.

Remember, in many cases this is the number 1 thing you can do to immediately improve your marriage. And I wasn't kidding—it is cheaper than therapy or divorce. Just think of it as preventative medicine.

Honestly, how can you expect your marriage to run on no gas? If you are not spending regular *fun* time together, you are running on fumes. I find it interesting that most families can find the time for driving the kids to soccer or Scouts or whatever myriad of activities they're involved in, and yet don't find the time for each other.

David K. Whitmer, a marriage counselor for over thirty years, advises us, "Continue to date each other throughout your marriage. I am very serious when I tell my Preparing for Marriage classes: 'Dating may be more important after marriage than it is before.' A couple needs to spend time alone together on a regular basis. I was impressed with Richard and Merilynne Linford's testimonial in the *Ensign* some years ago. They wrote, 'Time together doesn't have to be purely for recreation. We have read to each other from such sources as a child development book, a Church history book, the *Ensign,* a book on business management, and the Book of Mormon. We have also painted a room or done other odd jobs.' (*Ensign,* July 1976, p. 45.)

"After the marriage ceremony, cultural forces in modern society work to separate husband and wife. Overcommitment outside the home can rob the marriage relationship. Children can become not only sweet and precious, but also manipulative, demanding more and more time. So most couples will need to make time to be alone.

"In my counseling practice, I often tell parents, 'Your kids need a break from you once in a while.' My wife often counsels couples in workshops that 'baby-sitters may be the best investment you will ever make for your relationship. Baby-sitters are much less expensive than marriage counselors.'"[3] Said by a true expert—and a smart husband.

Now there are some rules to really make this a great experience.

Rule 1—Observe the 50 percent conversation limit.

Here's the rule: When you go on a date, 50 percent or more of your conversations have to be about something other than the kids. That may be a challenge at first. You can talk about current events, projects you're working on, finances, or whatever. But no more than half about kids. That requires you to take off your "Mommy" and "Daddy" hats and become "Hot Husband" and "Wonder Wife."

Rule 2—Don't get in a rut.

A fun-living wife is creative. This is your chance to let those creative juices flow. If your dates have devolved into dinner and Wal-Mart every week, it's time to perk them up!

You can get some great ideas on the internet. But do be careful. You can imagine what might pop up if you don't have a good filter. It may be best to put in "LDS" or "Christian" when doing a search! Talk to other people to get ideas. Look in the activity section of your local paper. Another idea to help save money and give you something fun to do is to buy movie passes in bulk. Many theaters will give you tickets much cheaper if you do this. Our theater sells them for half price if you buy fifty at a time. In the past, we would go in with a bunch of couples and buy them this way. Now with all our teenagers, we pretty well go through them with just our family. So call the theater and ask.

Also, having double or triple dates is a lot of fun. We set that up about once every other month. There is a sad side effect to this. Invariably when we go out on such a date, one of the couples will say, "Gee, the last time we went out was with you guys." Oh, how sad is that! They're dating us as much as their spouse!

Rule 3—Remember, you're on a *date*.

Now I admit that I have to remind myself of this on occasion. Sometimes I get casual and think, "Eh, these jeans look fine. And that ketchup stain from lunch on my shirt is barely noticeable." I have to smack myself at this point and remember that I'm going on a date. And if I were single and dating, I would not be caught dead in mother-homemaker clothes. So I have to dress up in my cute date-night duds.

So get yourself all gussied up. Do your hair. Throw on some lip gloss (and tell him, "Ummm, I'm wearing strawberry gloss. You'll have to try it!"). And throw on some perfume. Brush those pearly whites. And away you go.

You also have to remember date-night decorum. Sit in the car until he lets you out. (I'm so terrible at this part. I'm always impatient.) Say nice things. Compliment him. Ask about his day and his week.

Just close your eyes and think back—for some of us *way* back—and you'll remember what it was like. Enjoy.

Rule 4—No dumping allowed.

This is a date, and it is not the time for you to do an emotional dump. I know you've had a stressful week and you finally have his undivided attention. You'd love to complain about the neighbors, how the kids are driving you crazy, why your latest diet isn't working, and how you're retaining water. But now is not the time. Just think what would happen on a date if you were single and you performed a massive unloading. He'd run for the hills without your phone number in tow. Your husband wants to spend time with his smart wife who looks great, smells great, and says sweet things into his ear. He needs to leave the "mother" at home. You need to leave her there as well.

Rule 5—Enjoy the courting.

Have fun! You're still courting him and getting him to fall in love with you all the time. So have fun and be fun. Be attractive. Dazzle him. And stare into those beautiful eyes you fell in love with, and thank your lucky stars you got him.

In an article called "Keeping Your Marriage Alive," Paul Dahl tells of a marriage that was on the rocks. He was a priesthood leader and was consulted to help. He was shocked, as he had thought it was a solid marriage. He said, "As we talked, I concluded that they were both doing adequate jobs in their roles as father and mother, but that they hadn't spent enough time and effort on their own relationship.

"In their twenty years of marriage, Bill and Sharon had usually included others in their activities, especially their children. But very seldom did just the two of them spend time together. They emphasized children's birthdays, but not each other's. When Christmas arrived, most of the gifts were for the children; this was also true of other occasions during the year. Yes, they were involved as parents, but they were neglecting each other. Even when they went to dinner it was always with another couple. And when Bill expressed his feelings about Sharon's personal grooming, she responded, 'There was never enough time or money after providing for the children's needs!'

"She then expressed feelings of being ignored and never really feeling important in her husband's eyes. 'In fact,' she stated, 'I have felt just like another one of the children.'"[4]

That's interesting, because often I hear the *husbands* say that they feel like just another one of the kids and that their wives treat them like that. In fact, recently I asked a woman how many children she had. She replied, "I'm married and I have one daughter—so I have a boy and a girl." I chuckled but I also cringed a bit.

Let's take the time to treat each other as husband and wife at least once a week.

The Couple That Plays Together Stays Together

Playing together is crucial as a couple. There were certain things you did when dating that helped get you together. Those things cannot die in a marriage, or your marriage will begin to die as well.

149

So you want to live it up and have fun? Let's go to it.

Think of those shared experiences you have. Were they while you were skiing, or snorkeling, or reading books, or listening to country music?

Let's look at where you are now. Write down three things that the two of you do together now. Remember, breathing does not count! And make sure they are fun things. (I can see you now: "Well, let's see, we were scrubbing the grout together last Saturday. Does that count?" No!)

Now add to that list what you did when you were courting. Every couple has its own unique list. Sue and Kyle are total sci-fi buffs. Hilda and Roger loved to dance and travel. Marty and Karen loved backpacking. Linda and Kenny are campers and rock hounds. Kathe and Dennis loved everything having to do with the beach. Each of us will have our own list. Do you remember them? Are you still doing them?

What interests do you share? My husband and I both love Scouting. Our friends just adore Tom Clancy books. Some couples are history buffs. Others are really into politics. So what are your interests? You might include things that interest you, even though you don't currently have any shared activities reflecting those interests. But once you realize you have these things in common, you can come up with ways to have fun together while pursuing those interests.

And what's wrong with football? Go ahead and list those things that he likes and add those things that you like. Even though football may not ring your chimes, you can agree to go once in a while. (But I must admit that I find baseball extraordinarily boring and have been known to sneak in a book. Steve doesn't really love it either, though, so we've pretty well given that one up.) And once in a while, Steve can be convinced to walk through the art museum with me, once he is properly fed.

But it is important to have at least one activity on your list

150

that's physical. For some reason, doing something physical together spices things up and keeps you young. So what activity will you pick? We've talked about a lot of them. Just pick one! And it's okay if you don't do it well. Unless you're in the Olympics, no one will be pulling out those rating cards to judge your performance.

I will never forget Lynn. Lynn was—how should I say this delicately—a large woman. We had a big pool party and here comes Lynn wrapped in a muumuu. But then she took it off, revealed a new and stylish bathing suit, and went right into the pool. And Lynn's skinny husband went in after her. They had a great time, splashing and swimming and hugging. And I was taught a great lesson. Who cares that Lynn was bigger than average? Her husband sure didn't. And I was so proud of her for getting in there and mixing it up with everyone else.

Contrast that with Veronica, who has put on weight and over the years has given up every single physical thing she and her husband ever did. She just keeps putting on more weight and never gets out to move or do anything with her husband.

The couple that plays together keeps their marriage vibrant and alive and growing. Think about it. What will you do when the kids are gone? What will you talk about? What will you do together? Time flies really fast. Here I am only four years away from having the kids moving out and I'm shocked. My brain is still twenty-five, and shortly it'll be just the two of us. Wow! It will happen to you quickly as well. So what will you have in common? What fun can you have? Start now.

As I mentioned before, I have seen many couples split up because the husband looks across the table at his wife and thinks, "Well, we really don't do anything together. We don't have any fun anymore." And they begin to look elsewhere.

Wouldn't you rather have your husband look across that table and think, "Man, she sure is fun to be with. When the kids are gone, we are going to travel and water-ski and go antiquing. We are going to have a blast. I can't wait!" Now that's a fun-*living* wife!

So have you established connections with your husband that have nothing to do with your children? Or do you have a parallel marriage? You know what I'm talking about. You've seen them. The wife goes about her day mothering and shopping and cleaning and spending time with her friends and really has no connection to her husband other than to discuss his paycheck. And the husband goes about his day working and reading the paper and going with his buddies to the game and really has no connection to his wife other than to ask when dinner will be ready. They live parallel lives with few connections. And once the big connections (i.e., the children) move out, they have so few ties left that they are easily severed.

If you are living a parallel existence, now is the time to fix it. You can begin today to establish some connections to have fun together. It is crucial to do this now.

Unfortunately, the couple that does *not* play together may not stay together.

Now part of being a fun-living wife is also to be just plain fun. Take responsibility for generating your own fun. It's not your husband's job to entertain you. As I described earlier in the book, I was asked an important question by a psychologist: "Do you expect your husband to meet all your emotional needs?" I realized that that was an unfair burden and began to take care of myself.

Being a fun-living wife requires you to get in touch with what *you* find fun. Some women may think that that's a pretty stupid comment. Others are like me and struggle with this. I am such a workaholic that I have to really give this thought. I can remember years ago when we had so many little ones and my husband would say, "Why don't you go do something fun, and I'll take care of the kids." And I'd stand there and think, "Gee, what should I do?" My idea of fun was to go to the grocery store by myself. Ugh! It took a lot of effort for me to connect again with the "fun" in me and find things that would be enjoyable.

So while you're making a "couples fun" list, make one of your own. And have at it.

A fun-living wife will mix it up. Have fun with your husband. Have fun with your girlfriends. Pursue your interests.

I have fun with politics. I know, that's a weird one. But I love it. I love getting in a crowded room of people and working the room. I love going door-to-door and working on causes and campaigns. Doing this is like having a root canal to my husband. But he knows I love it and totally supports me. (In fact, he was my biggest supporter in my campaign and did many things that were very challenging to him, which I so appreciate.) Sue loves to do tole painting. Her supportive husband built her an entire craft room. She's so happy creating and painting. And her husband loves the fact that she's fun and creative.

Having fun with your friends is a great outlet as well. We go to all the restaurants our husbands hate and go see chick flicks together and go shopping and talk, talk, talk. When we come home, we are all hyped up and our husbands benefit from having *very* fun-living wives!

Keep Being Alluring

The smart wife is alluring. No doubt about it. She was able to attract that great husband, and she never takes for granted that the attraction phase is over.

How can we be alluring? I would suggest three things: be mysterious, be unpredictable, be spontaneous.

Be mysterious. Sometimes men are attracted to mysterious women. The unknown is very alluring. So be mysterious. Give him those dreamy-eyed, mysterious, alluring looks. You don't need to keep secrets from your husband, but you also don't need to gush out every single thing going on in your head! Play with this a bit. Have fun with it. He'll love it.

Be unpredictable. This is a little challenging if you're a mother. How unpredictable can you be when the children rise at 6:30 A.M., breakfast is served, kids get dressed, go to school at 7:30 A.M., you read your scriptures, clean the house, run your errands, feed the toddler at noon, naptime at 12:30 P.M., kids home at 2:30 P.M., and on you go in your highly scheduled day. But if you keep this in your head, you can find little ways that will surprise him. Once in a while say, "I'm dying to go to a football game!" Pause while he pulls his jaw back up off the floor. Occasionally just stop and say, "You know what, you're absolutely right!" That'll keep him on his toes! Wear something slinky to bed on a Wednesday. Wake up on Saturday and make him brownies and ice cream for breakfast. Have fun being unpredictable. He will find your sometimes being unpredictable to be alluring!

Be spontaneous. If we thought being unpredictable was a challenge, being spontaneous can be even harder. Just remember Stop, Drop, and Roll. (You thought that was just for putting yourself out when you've caught fire. Not so!) To be spontaneous, *stop* what you are doing. Go ahead. Stop making dinner. Stop the phone call. Stop scrubbing the toilet. Then *drop* everything. Yup. Drop your plans to vacuum the carpet edges. Drop the tax returns you were working on. Drop everything. And *roll* with it!

Your husband says, "Honey, do you want to go sit in the Jacuzzi?" You don't say, "Well, gee, my hair may get wet and I don't like my bathing suit and what about this electric bill I need to pay . . . blah, blah, blah." You say, "You bet!" You dash upstairs, throw on the suit, race downstairs, and jump in.

Or perhaps you see him out there playing badminton with the kids. Stop doing the dishes. Drop the dish towel, and roll out that door and join them. Be spontaneous.

Now you're wondering, how can I be spontaneous when everything I do involves lining up a sitter? Ah, there is a solution. I call this *planned spontaneity.* You understand that you need to be alluring. You understand that part of this is being a spontaneous, fun-living wife. So you plan it out. You line up the sitter for a Tuesday night (now *that's* spontaneous) and say to your husband that night, "You know what, much as I love eating tuna casserole with the kids, let's just ditch this joint right now." Tell him he has five minutes to get ready. Grab the sitter and bomb out the door. He'll be stunned. He'll be sitting there in the movie theater watching the latest action flick he wanted to see and thinking, "Man, how did we end up here? My wife is incredible. I never thought she'd go see this with me and she just dropped everything." You'll be positively irresistible!

Now that you're mysterious, unpredictable, and spontaneous, you still need to do something else: flirt shamelessly. Many of us did that to attract a mate years ago. It's still popular. Bring it back! You, too, can and should flirt shamelessly—just make sure you limit it to your husband! Flirting with your husband is a blast. And frankly, it takes ten years off your brain. Stare at him across the room. Lick your lips. Pat him on the knee. Make flirty comments. Have fun with this!

Let us compare. You are out to dinner at the restaurant. "Honey, we have got to get at that mold problem in the bathroom. It's creeping me out. And, oh, there's Marybeth and Neil. She drives me crazy. Did you know that they had a lice outbreak in their family? Well, anyway, don't forget you need to take the kids to that service project. They said to bring work gloves and a shovel. Oh, these pants are killing me. I think I ate too much." Oh, my. I'm getting grossed out and I'm not even married to this woman. And I have heard these kinds of conversations more than I care to!

On the other hand, a woman who is trying to be alluring would conduct her date-night conversation thusly. You are out to dinner at the restaurant. You say, "Have we met? You look familiar." (He stares back, wondering what you're drinking.) You reach out and stroke his lips. "My, but you *are* handsome. What did you say your name was? I was hoping that you'd ask me out." You stroke his hand. You smile a dazzling smile. "What are you doing later on?" And she goes on from there.

Now who was having a good time? Let's all vote for wife number 2. You may have been giggling on the inside, but I can bet that he was hooked! He's thinking, "Oh, baby, my wife *is* the perfect wife!"

So have fun flirting shamelessly. He'll love it and so will you.

Now part of being alluring is to keep yourself attractive. I've discussed this a lot before, so just a few pointers. One tip: discover beauty colleges! Talk about cheap beauty. You can find them everywhere, and they can be a very inexpensive way to help you stay attractive. Now that I'm over forty, I wanted to maintain my face a little better, so I go to the beauty college about every eight weeks for a facial and waxing. (Okay, men aren't the only ones that grow weird hair as they age.) I get an hour of heaven for about $10. Cannot beat it! Also, try to keep in style. You don't have to wear the latest stomach-baring fashions. But look at your closet and make sure the vast majority of your clothing was purchased during this millennium. Remember the Dork Test. Finally, add items that make you feel attractive and that enhance your natural beauty. Remember to occasionally (spontaneously!) spice it up. Spice adds flavor. So get your toes painted red and wear high-heeled sandals instead of last year's flip-flops. You get the idea . . .

Remember, the smart wife continues to be alluring.

Go on a Honeymoon—Again!

Remember number 9 in the Top Ten List? That's right. Was your last overnight away together to attend a funeral? I picked this because I had an actual woman come up to me and try to rationalize that she spent time with her husband because they had gone away to attend a funeral. Not my idea of a hot week-end together.

So think, when was the last time you got away together—even if it was just for one night? It may have been a long time. I remember attending a Rotary meeting last year, and one of the men stood up during the "confessions" time of the meeting and announced that he and his wife were going away on a cruise. And then he explained that it was the first time in thirty years that they would have gone away together. He got a big fine for that one! He happens to be a friend of mine, so I read him the riot act afterward.

Talk about killing your marriage. Eek! That sounds like piti-ful boredom. A fun-living wife plots and plans to go away on an overnighter at least once a year. As your kids get older and finances improve, this can increase (my sister goes away monthly!). But for now, let's set a goal to go at least once a year.

Oh, I can just hear you now. The excuses are just spilling out, aren't they? You should know by now that those just won't work. We're becoming smart wives, not boring wives with per-fect excuses. No way.

So save your quarters if you have to, but go away. I say that literally. My mom decided that she wanted to go to Europe, so she began saving her quarters. She saved her quarters for years and was finally able to afford the trip.

Again, you can be creative. Trade baby-sitting with another couple or ask a young married couple to come and stay the night. They are usually very willing. Or get Mom to come and pray she cleans while she's there. Watch for ads and specials. The internet is full of great deals—especially last-minute ones. Ask your parents to give you gift certificates for Christmas to restaurants and the like rather than another sweater. You can go camping very cheaply (I am at my happiest in a tent!).

You may need to start out simple and just take an entire day away. But start! And if you have to absolutely bring the nursing baby, that's okay. Go anyway. (But that's the only time kids are invited.)

It can be short; it can be close by; but leave!

It is amazing what a short time away can do to rejuvenate your marriage. So go ahead and take that mini-honeymoon every year. It is absolutely worth every penny. It's worth all the arranging, all the planning, and all the effort. And it will take a lot of effort! Do it anyway.

Your husband will be so grateful that his smart wife made the effort. And you'll fall in love all over again.

Be a Fun-Living Wife

A big part of being a fun-living wife is making it a part of every day and a part of your basic personality. The first step is awareness. So ask yourself, "Are we having fun yet?" If you're aware, you can tell if the marriage is getting stale. Have things become just routine? Is it, dare I say it, boring? You'll know if it is.

So it helps to occasionally take the marriage temperature. You can gauge if things need a little kicking up if you pay attention.

And if you take your marital temperature and find that things are running a little too cool, consider adding some spice.

In Paul Dahl's article "Keeping Your Marriage Alive" (remember Bill and Sharon?), he also recommended that they do something special for the other person every day. He said the couple was "so far apart in meeting each other's needs that they did not know where to begin. . . . [Sharon] said, 'If I baked you a pecan pie, would that be something special?'

"Bill exclaimed, 'Would that be special! You've never baked a pecan pie. You've always felt we couldn't afford it.'

"Then he asked, 'Would it be special if I took you to the stake sweetheart dance next week?'

"She started to cry and said, 'I didn't think we would ever go to a dance again.'"[5]

Special little things can make a world of difference. And you can start today. Let's talk about some things you could do. How about giving him treats? We give treats to our kids but rarely if ever think of giving something to our spouse. One Valentine's Day I got my husband a mug with candy and a teddy bear with a mylar balloon sticking out of it. Man, he kept that thing on his desk for years. It was collecting dust and I finally said, "Honey, why don't you get rid of that?" He was horrified. "What, no way! I love that!"

There are a ton of little treats that would really mean a lot to your hubby: candy (what man can resist Snickers bars? My ward gives out huge Snickers bars on Father's Day. The guys love them!), a big balloon, a funny card, a Hawaiian girl air freshener for his car, sunglasses, a pool toy, a really nice beach towel, a little bowl with a goldfish, a new key ring—I could go on and on. And for those of you who actually cook and bake—well, you have it made in the shade! Warm chocolate chip cookies are huge. (Feel free to ship me some c/o Deseret Book. I'm sure I'll get them.) My husband would do cartwheels for brownies.

A well-timed treat can work wonders. Don't give them out in any regular or predictable fashion. Just every once in a while here and there. But a little treat can perk things up and make him feel loved and appreciated. He'll think you're wonderful.

Surprises are also fun. Meet him for lunch. Drop off a treat at his office. Kidnap him for the weekend. Arrange for a weekend with his buddies and spring it on him. Remember to keep him on his toes! He'll love it.

It's also important to keep the "silly" in a marriage. Remember the stupid, silly stuff you did when you were younger? Resurrect it! One day our family was sitting in Burger King and I announced, "Let's have a Weird Body Parts Contest." Now we had never done this before, but we quickly learned that we have multitalented family members who can do amazing things with parts of their bodies. From wiggling ears to flaring nostrils (my youngest is gifted!), we were laughing like crazy. (Our apologies to those of you who frequent the Burger King near the copper mine in Utah.) But Parker won the prize. He could ruffle-fold his tongue in his mouth into four sections. It was pure genius. Who knew?

My poor husband and children know that I love to be silly. They'll say, "Mom, you're weird."

I say, "Gee thanks! I try to be!" (One day, one of my son's friends said to him, "Your mom is really weird." "I know," my son replied, "but don't tell her that. She thinks it's a big compliment.") Sometimes we get so bogged down in the whole "responsible parent" routine that we forget to lighten up and be silly. This is especially true with our husbands.

You can write funny poems:

> *There was an old woman who lived in a shoe*
> *She gained so many pounds she didn't know what to do.*
> *So she ate broth and good whole-grained bread,*
> *Whipped her body into shape*
> *And turned every head!*
>
> *There was an old woman who once lived in a shoe*
> *But she read this whole book and learned what to do.*

She became quite amazing with all that she read
And moved into a high-heel
With the husband she wed.

Have fun! Be silly! Your husband will be kept guessing and wonder what's come over you. But he will appreciate the younger, sillier you.

Part of being a fun-living wife every day is to do all those sweet little things that make a marriage grow. Every night for years my husband would say when we got into bed, "Honey, would you like a kiss?"

"Why yes, I would," I would reply.

At that point, he would hand me one Hershey's kiss. It was our own little, ongoing joke. (And frankly, ending the day with a tiny bit of chocolate didn't hurt!)

For a very long time, my husband and I would take turns bringing each other breakfast in bed. He'd serve me on Saturdays, and I'd serve him on Sundays. It was a sweet gesture that meant a lot.

So think of sweet things you can do. I'll list a few that I've observed others doing: putting a love note in his suit pocket; kissing him on the nose; saying every day, "Boy, am I glad I married you!"; folding down his bed at night; turning on the Jacuzzi so it's warm when he comes back from a hike; putting little hearts in his sock drawer; playing "your song" in the car; giving him a big lingering hug—you name it.

Those sweet things are like adding sunshine to flowers. It helps things bloom. As we get swept up in the requirements of daily living, these things often get swept by the wayside. A woman writing of the change in her marriage wrote, "An elderly friend added his gift of wisdom to our formula: 'Think of marriage as if it were an empty jar, waiting to be filled,' he said. 'Each act of kindness places a spoonful of sugar into it; every selfish act takes one out. At the end of each year, will your jar be empty or overflowing? Your marriage, bitter or sweet?'"[6]

Elder Dean L. Larsen discussed this in his talk "Enriching Marriage": "Don't become too casual in your relationship with each other. Don't overlook the common courtesies, even when you are alone and others will not see. This includes the 'may I's,' the 'pleases,' the 'thank yous,' and sometimes, when necessary, the 'I'm sorrys.' It means you regularly express the necessary endearments that have to be expressed if those feelings that bind you together are to be nurtured, fostered, and strengthened. One of our married daughters expresses it this way: 'Don't always be predictable.' And by that she simply means, do some unusual things occasionally.

"I suppose it wouldn't be inappropriate for me to share an experience I had with my wife. As I returned home one afternoon from a stake conference in Salt Lake City, I found that Sister Larsen had prepared a wonderful meal. The table was set with our best china and the silverware that we usually use only when guests are present. It was special. That doesn't happen every day or even every Sunday or it wouldn't be special. But those are the kinds of things that can add greatly to a bond of love and companionship that will endure."[7] Ah, and Elder Larsen liked his unpredictable wife, didn't he?

Being a fun-living, smart wife every day means that you don't forget the little tiny things that make a marriage sweet. We expect him to be romantic, but what do we do to treat him like a prince? Adding these little things takes more mental effort than anything else. And it will perk up a stale marriage rather quickly.

Luckily, Steve doesn't like pecan pie, but he does like Snickers.

Shared "Codes"—Developing Connections

I like a story told by the daughter of President and Sister Hugh B. Brown: "Up until Mother's stroke they'd go through a ritual daily. Daddy would get up from the breakfast table that Mother had set very nicely, with a pretty cloth, matching napkins, and flowers. He'd kiss her good-bye and then they would walk to the front porch together.

"Daddy would go down three steps, and then turn around and ask, 'Did I kiss you good-bye?' Mother would answer, 'Why, no, you didn't.' Daddy would kiss her again.

"As he walked to the car, Mother would run into the dining room where she would blow kisses to him from the window. While Daddy was backing the car out of the drive, Mother would run back to the porch where she'd wave a handkerchief until he drove out of sight.

"Just before the car turned the corner, Daddy would blink the brake lights three times, his code for 'I love you.'"[8]

What a sweet connection of love they had developed! What a tender thing they shared each day.

We can establish our own connections. I call these "shared codes." They're the little communications you have between the two of you. They can be sweet like my friend's husband who honks his horn three times as he's leaving for work. And they can be not so subtle like kicking you in the leg under the table to signal you that you're getting close to the line. But they are connections just between you and your husband, whether they're signals, certain phrases, or whatever you use.

BYU professor E. Jeffrey Hill spoke at a recent BYU Women's Conference of a sweet connection he had with his wife: "This campus will always hold a special place in my heart. This is where I met, courted, and married my wife of twenty-nine years, Juanita Ray Hill. One particular memory of that era stands out in my mind. I wanted to present my future wife with an engagement ring in an out-of-the-ordinary location. So while riding the Wilkinson Center elevator I surprised her with a glittering diamond, the symbol of my affection. In delight, she threw her arms around me and gave me a *very* affectionate hug and kiss, right up to, and even a little after, the elevator doors opened wide at the Sky Room. What an exciting moment!

"Ever since then, Juanita and I have had the tradition of embracing and kissing in elevators. When others were riding with us I would just give her a discrete tap on the shoulder and a peck on the cheek. But when we would find ourselves alone we re-created those romantic feelings of young love with very affectionate hugs and kisses. My, how I like elevators!"[9] What a dear love was expressed in that shared experience. It still brought Brother Hill comfort after his wife passed away.

My daddy had a signal that he used throughout his life. As he got older, he shared this with virtually every child he ever saw. He'd stop to talk to a little child and he'd say, "Do you want me to teach you a secret?" The child would usually stare up at my dad with big eyes. He'd hold up his first finger and say, "Now you hold up your finger like this and you wave it up and down three times." He'd help the child to imitate him. Then he'd say, "Now you have the secret. So when you see your mommy across the room, you just wave your finger three times and that means, 'I love you.'"

Just the week before Daddy died, we all shared the sweetest, dearest moment when he waved his finger to his sweet grandchildren and great-grandchildren. Our family will always treasure our secret signal.

So what is your code for "I love you"? You can use three of anything to signal that to your husband. Make up your own. What is your signal for "Okay, I'm done and it's time to go"? With us, one of us will say, "Well, it's time to go check if the house has burned down." Now I'm sure that many hostesses wondered if this was literal, with four sons at home. (It probably started out that way!) What is your signal for "I'm bored out of my gourd"? Or "You're embarrassing me to death"? My poor husband has to use that code quite a bit. The other day I was so dense. I was talking to the missionaries, who were over for dinner. (I get pizza for them every time. Saves my sanity.) So he's kicking me and I say, "Are you kicking my leg to get me to shut up, or are you negotiating for more room under there?" Poor dear, I'm subtle as a brick.

Having little shared codes and signals helps connect you together as a married couple.

Also think about how you handle arrivals and departures. When your husband comes home, does he get a bigger reaction from the dog than he does from you? Acknowledging his coming home and leaving is a significant thing; it can do a lot to solidify your feelings for each other. A fun-living, smart wife makes a big deal out of this. For years my husband would call out when he came home, "Oh, Luuuucy, I'm home!" in a thick Spanish accent. (Okay, for you young pups, that's from an old TV show with Lucille Ball.) And I'd give him a big hug and kiss.

This one's harder now because my husband and I both work at home. I have to consciously remember to make a big deal out of it because we're always coming and going with our jobs. But it's still important and worth giving attention to.

Now remember the Seesaw Principle? I talked about how marriages seek to reach equilibrium. Another facet of this is that emotional intensity goes up and down as well. Sometimes your marriage will be hot and spicy. Other times it will be comfortable like flannel jammies. Sometimes it will be really fun and energetic and other times quiet and close. It's okay. Just stay on the seesaw and enjoy the ride.

NOTES

1. Spencer W. Kimball, "Marriage and Divorce," *1976 Devotional Speeches of the Year* (Provo, Utah: Brigham Young University Press, 1977), 150, 146.

2. Barbara Workman, "Love, Laughter, and Spirituality in Marriage," *Ensign,* July 1992, 7.

3. David K. Whitmer, "Return to the Honeymoon Place," *Ensign,* January 1991, 61–62.

4. Paul E. Dahl, "Keeping Your Marriage Alive," *Ensign,* July 1982, 56.

5. Dahl, "Keeping Your Marriage Alive," 59.

6. Judith Long, "The Formula That Saved Our Marriage," *Ensign,* March 1983, 17.

7. Dean L. Larsen, "Enriching Marriage," *Ensign,* March 1985, 21–22.

8. *Church News,* 26 October 1974, 5.

9. E. Jeffrey Hill, "Meeting Family Challenges Together," BYU Women's Conference, April 28–29, 2005; unpublished transcript.

CHAPTER 8

Becoming a Smart Wife Yourself

*Persevere through it all, and with all your good
and faithful effort, you will have grown and become a
truly smart wife in the process.*

B y now you're a fun-living wife, and both you and your husband are on the road to working on a great marriage. In this last chapter, I will add just a few concepts to help you go forward to that wifely perfection of being a completely smart wife, which lurks just over the horizon.

Sense of Humor

As you work on becoming a smart wife over the next few months and years—and, well, probably decades—it will go a lot smoother if you have a sense of humor. Don't bother to take yourself too seriously—no one else does!

Sister Chieko Okazaki tells us to "Lighten Up!" I decided if I wrote a book on the topic, I would call it, "Chill Out!" I'm sure it would be a bestseller.

There are a gazillion articles and books written on what husbands expect or want in their wives. But if there were one written on what they hope for, I believe that sense of humor would be right at the top of the list (well, right after long hair and the ability to cook well).

Men love women who laugh. And a woman who can laugh at herself and at life is a true jewel.

So when you are dropping your husband off and you absent-mindedly jump out of the car in your jammies, carefully locking your side, and he jumps out and just as carefully locks his side—and the car is running and it's winter—you just have to laugh. And you keep laughing as you run into the building to get a coat hanger—only to discover that all the hangers are attached to the rod . . . and the car is still running. Just keep laughing.

President James E. Faust agrees, "There is . . . a defense against adversity: humor. . . .

"For many years as I have blessed newborn children, including my own, I have blessed them with a sense of humor. [Interestingly, I asked my husband to be open to an impression to do this as well when he was blessing our babies. I figured they would sure need it.] I do this with the hope that it will help guard them against being too rigid, that they will have balance in their lives, and that situations and problems and difficulties will not be overdrawn. . . .

"Our leaders have demonstrated that one can enjoy both faith and humor. It was said of President Heber C. Kimball (1801–68) that he prayed and conversed with God 'as one man talketh with another' (Abr. 3:11). However, 'on one occasion, while offering up an earnest appeal in behalf of certain of his fellow creatures, he startled the kneeling circle by bursting into a loud laugh in the very midst of his prayer. Quickly regaining his composure and solemn address, he remarked, apologetically, 'Lord, it makes me laugh to pray about some people' (Orson F. Whitney, *Life of Heber C. Kimball* [1992], 427). . . .

"A good sense of humor will help us hone our talents. One

of the talents that needs to be greatly magnified is sensitivity to others, and this involves reaching out and touching another heart. By learning not to be afraid ourselves, we are able to stir up kindred feelings for others. Under the cultivation of the Holy Ghost, our talents become greatly magnified."[1]

One of the things we all love about our dear prophet is his sense of humor. He never takes himself too seriously—which is surprising since he is the *prophet* of the entire world, and that's a pretty serious thing! But you can tell that he and his wife have lived their lives with humor. Sister Hinckley always had that twinkle in her eye.

A healthy sense of humor in a wife is like a good lubricant for the family and the marriage. Everything just goes much more smoothly. I must admit that it never ceases to amaze me how serious Mormon women are. It's no wonder there's a depression problem.

Learn to poke fun at yourself while you're at it. This takes a certain level of confidence, but it works wonders. In our ward Relief Society, I have made it clearly known that I am seriously cooking-impaired. When they pass out the paper for sign-ups, they all comment that obviously I will be assigned paper products. I am the Paper-Product Queen! The last time I baked for a Cub Scout Blue and Gold banquet, sometime in the 1990s, I made cupcakes that totally fell—as in oozing over the edges. I don't know why people had a problem with cupcakes that were flat with crispy edges, but only one poor soul even ventured to eat one. My children announced in quite a loud voice as we were cleaning up that I was forbidden to bake ever again and that they would do the baking from then on. So when it is announced in Relief Society that we need baked goods, I cheerily announce, "Great! I'll tell the kids!" Now the truth of the matter is that I'm really not that horrible of a cook. But you'd never know it. We have way too much fun making a big joke out of it.

If you can chill out and look at the funny side of things, your husband and everyone else will feel a whole lot more comfortable. Nothing can break the tension more than that. So when you're arguing with your husband and yelling at him and find that you're spitting mad, stop and have fun. Spit some more. Cross your eyes. And then go ahead and have a belly laugh. He will love you for it.

And if you'll laugh at my jokes, you can come party with me anytime!

Continue Growing and Evolving

Now obviously you are the poster child for this concept—you're still reading!

Think of a stagnant pond of water. What happens to it? It gets murkier and murkier. It begins to grow a green scum. It attracts flies—lots of flies. The plants inside start to die and the whole thing begins to devolve into a pile of dark green sludge.

Now think of a woman who has become stagnant in her progression. Very similar, isn't it? Her personality becomes murkier and murkier. She, hopefully, doesn't grow green scum but her appearance begins to degenerate. She repels lively people and attracts negative people. And things don't improve.

One of the absolute hallmarks of a smart wife is that she continues to grow and to evolve. By evolve, I mean that she changes and adapts and improves. By nature of our culture, LDS women tend to do well in this regard.

Look back on the last ten years and review your own personal life and development. Have you improved your behavior? Do you have success? Have you changed those things that are no longer helpful or positive?

I think the one danger that we do face is that of mediocrity. I'd like to repeat a statement I used earlier from President

Hinckley: "I have been quoted as saying, 'Do the best you can.' But I want to emphasize that it be the very best. We are too prone to be satisfied with mediocre performance. We are capable of doing so much better."[2]

It is a constant challenge to keep ourselves growing and improving. We spend so much time helping everyone else in our lives in their growing and improving that we sometimes put ourselves at the bottom of the to-do list.

This relates to one of the big complaints I hear from couples who split up after many years of marriage. Often the husband will say, "She just didn't change. The kids grew up and left and she was just the same mother-type woman." They see a woman who didn't improve her appearance or didn't improve her mind or just didn't come to grips with the fact that her family was changing and she needed to change along with it.

Often young mothers get sidetracked on this very early. They begin having babies and set aside all of their own growth, putting it in their mental cedar chest and covering it in mothballs. I've heard the comments they make over and over, "Well, when the kids are grown, I plan to . . . " Fill in the blank. I always say, "Why wait?" No one is asking you (or even wanting you) to put your life on hold. Now granted, you may not be able to do everything you want to do at this particular stage in your life, but you can do something.

You want to read more? Do it now. You want to start that exercise program? Do it now. You want to learn more about the scriptures? Today is a good day to start. Putting off growth and evolution is like procrastinating "the day of your salvation," as the scriptures say. You could reach a point where "it is everlastingly too late" (Helaman 13:38). If you keep putting it off, you will be too tired or too old or too lazy or too whatever and never get around to it.

Every single husband on the planet (if he's wise) wants a wife who is going for it. He wants to be proud of her. He wants to come home every day to hear of something new that she did or learned. He wants a wife he can brag about. You can be that wife. He already loves you. He also wants to be stimulated by your growing and changing and be interested in you.

It is always interesting to talk to Elizabeth. To be honest, I was a little jealous of her. Elizabeth got both her law degree and her master's in public administration. I wanted that but didn't do it because I got married and figured I had better just finish law school. She had a really cool job as an FBI agent. How many FBI agent LDS women do you know? She was articulate and funny. You can tell I was very impressed.

Well, Elizabeth began to have children. Like everything else in her life, she did it fast! In four years she had three babies. I chuckled, "Aha, *now* let's see how she handles things." Elizabeth tackled motherhood the same way she tackled her career—with gusto! She studied motherhood and childrearing and education. She took her kids all over and began homeschooling them. Every time I run into her, she has some new thing to talk about. Now this is a woman who is constantly growing.

I'm not suggesting that you all need to go out and apply to the FBI. (Although that would be totally awesome: "Uh, sir. I'm not sure why, but we've had a rash of applications from LDS women. Do you think there's something going on?") What I am suggesting is that each of us can make sure that we are improving and learning and growing all the time.

It could be simple things. Libby's kids are getting older, so she now goes to the family history library each week to work on what she loves. Wendy loves to write. Even with four little boys at home, she is writing articles here and there. Sue took classes on the internet through BYU. Donna went back to school and finished her degree and is writing novels. Liza volunteers to help military families. Susan is doing yet another service mission.

Ellen is homeschooling her kids. Liesl is singing in the community choir. Stacy was the PTA president. Krystal took a class in flower arranging. Barbara started a new exercise regime (and is looking mighty fabulous). Jeana is becoming an expert at fancy chocolates (and we all appreciate her for it!). Denise is working on her piano skills. Jill got a new calling as provident living leader in our ward and is cooking each week from food storage and bringing it to Relief Society (we're *so* happy she got that calling!). Betsy is doing a ton of volunteer work with the humanitarian effort. I could go on and on. That's just a few of the women in my own ward who are growing and improving.

President Hinckley has repeatedly encouraged the women and wives of the Church to do their best to grow and develop. He said, "My wife likes to tell the story of a friend of hers who, when she was a little girl, was left an orphan. She scarcely knew her mother. As she grew, she wondered about her mother: what kind of a girl, what kind of a woman was she?

"One day she came across her mother's old report card. The teacher had noted on that card, 'This student is excellent in every way.'

"When she read that, her entire life changed. She recognized that her mother was a woman of excellence. Her whole attitude changed. She took on the aura of excellence herself and became a remarkable woman in her own right. She married a man who is recognized in many communities, and their children have distinguished themselves for their excellence.

"I speak of the need for a little more effort, a little more self-discipline, a little more consecrated effort in the direction of excellence in our lives.

"This is the great day of decision for each of us. For many it is the time of beginning something that will go on for as long as you live. I plead with you: don't be a scrub! Rise to the high ground of spiritual, mental, and physical excellence. You can do it. You may not be a genius. You may be lacking in some skills. But so many of us can do better than we are now doing. We are members of this great Church whose influence is now felt over the world. We are people with a present and with a future. Don't muff your opportunities. Be excellent."³

Perseverance

We have covered a lot of material in this book. I'm sure your head is just spinning with new entries for your "to-do" list. It would be easy to get discouraged and just say, "There's too much! I can't handle it!" Or you may be feeling that no matter what you do, you won't be a good wife, much less a really smart one. Or you may be convinced that nothing short of dropping a boulder on his head will ever get your husband's attention enough to change.

I have three words—*hang in there!*

Just pick one thing to work on and plug away at it. Keep trying. Pray for help. Write it down and keep persevering.

The Lord comforts us in Doctrine and Covenants 64:33: "Wherefore, be not weary in well-doing, for ye are laying the foundation of a great work. And out of small things proceedeth that which is great."

You may not notice the small things and you may not notice the small difference that is being made, but over time you will. Just keep working at it. Some of your years will be fantastic. Some years will be just okay. And some years will really try your spirit. Part of creating an eternal relationship is simply hanging in there through it all.

Barbara Workman has written: "Gerald Lund, a Church Educational System administrator [and now a General Authority], tells the story of medical personnel taking a truckload of supplies into the jungles of Africa to set up a hospital. The

174

bridges they had to cross were not strong enough to support the truck. Rather than lighten the load by leaving precious supplies behind, they stopped at each river or ravine to strengthen the bridge ("Strengthening the Bridges," Book of Mormon Symposium, Provo, Utah, 1986).

"When we set out to build a celestial marriage, we have no choice but to carry the whole load the whole way. We cannot drop off the heavy things, such as problems with children, financial burdens, or poor health. When we, in our problem-solving truck, reach a chasm, sometimes we must be willing to stop and strengthen the bridge for our marriage to get through."[4]

Persevere through it all. Just grit your teeth and carry on. And you will reach a point where you stop and look back at the trail that you've hiked and think, "Wow, we've made it through all of that. Look how well we're doing!" And hopefully, with all your good and faithful effort, you will have grown and become a truly smart wife in the process.

Help Him Become His Best

One husband shared this experience: "One spring day I came home in a cheerful mood, only to be met by my tearful wife. I quickly asked her what had happened. She replied that my father had called. This alarmed me because my father had disowned me some years earlier as a result of my activity in the Church. Feelings of anger stirred in my heart that he would call and upset my wife to the point of tears.

"My wife informed me that my father had tried to convince her of my inadequacies as a husband. Now I wanted to call my father to retaliate. However, I decided to wait and calm down first. For the next two days I remained angry and bitter. At the end of the second day, my wife and I knelt to pray. Since I did not feel in the right frame of mind to pray, I asked her if she would offer the prayer.

"She took my arm and said, 'Before we pray, I want you to read a scripture.' She turned to 3 Nephi and read: 'Love your enemies, bless them that curse you, do good to them that hate you, and pray for them who despitefully use you and persecute you' (3 Ne. 12:44).

"My heart began to pound. I felt suddenly as if the Savior were speaking directly to me because his words penetrated the deepest portion of my heart. Then I began to cry and felt my angry heart soften.

"When I looked at my wife, she said something I will never forget: 'Do you know why I gave you that scripture? I just want you to be the best person you can be.'

"I was overwhelmed. My sweet wife had opened a scriptural door that let the light of gospel principles shine through to my heart, and I was able to forgive my father. I came to appreciate my good wife even more. The gospel has given us a solid foundation in our marriage as we continue to help each other be the best we can be."[5]

This sweet story illustrates a key principle to becoming a great wife. You will be a great wife if you appropriately use all your efforts to help your husband become the son of God that he truly is. You can lift him up when he is down. You can encourage him to raise his behavior and standards to a higher level. You can comfort him and help him and love him. Through it all, your focus must be on helping him to be a better person. In the process, you, too, will become better for it.

God Bless You!

In closing, I would like to offer you my profoundest admiration and respect. First of all, congratulations on reading the whole thing! That shows your deep commitment to improving yourself as a wife, and that is very admirable. I know that the Lord will bless you for all of your sincere efforts and for the righteous desires of your heart.

I pray that each of us will be blessed with increased love in our hearts for our husbands. I hope that we will feel an increase of understanding and patience. And I pray that each of us will continue to grow and improve as wives so that someday we will be queens with our husbands, worthy to stand by their side, and that all our children and grandchildren and great-grandchildren and our posterity for generations will bless our names as righteous women.

I know that someday you will be the perfect wife. In the meantime, may you be blessed on your path to get there.

NOTES

1. James E. Faust, "The Need for Balance in Our Lives," *Ensign,* March 2000, 4, 5.
2. Gordon B. Hinckley, "Standing Strong and Immovable," *Worldwide Leadership Training Meeting,* 10 January 2004, 21.
3. Gordon B. Hinckley, "The Quest for Excellence," *Ensign,* September 1999, 4–5.
4. Barbara Workman, "Love, Laughter, and Spirituality in Marriage," *Ensign,* July 1992, 10.
5. Name withheld, "Building a Successful Marriage," *Ensign,* March 1998, 28; used by permission.

Index

About the Author

Merrilee Browne Boyack loves eating ice cream and taking naps. A popular speaker at BYU Education Week and Time Out for Women conferences, she has taught parenting and relationship principles to thousands. She is an estate-planning attorney who conducts her part-time law practice from her home in Poway, California.

Merrilee graduated with high honors from Brigham Young University with a degree in Business Management—Finance and was a summa cum laude graduate from the Santa Clara University Law School. She has four sons and a fabulous, supportive husband. She is a member of the Poway City Council; vice president of the local chapter and national board member of Mothers Without Borders; Rotary and Poway Chamber of Commerce member; and a community activist. She received the BYU Alumni Association Community Service Award and the PTA Council and Unit Honorary Service Award.

Merrilee's favorite kitchen appliance is a telephone. Her interests include reading, camping, talking, eating out, and riding her motorcycle. She is also the author of *The Parenting Breakthrough*.

You can contact Merrilee via email at mboyack@cox.net